A GREEN WITCH'S CUPBOARD

Also by Deborah J. Martin:

Herbs: Medicinal, Magical, Marvelous!

A Green Witch's Formulary

Baneful! 95 of the World's Worst Herbs

A Green Witch's Cupboard

Deborah J. Martin, M.H.

Copyright ©2015 Deborah J. Martin
Cover art by Kit Foster Design

ISBN: 978-0-9888547-6-5 (print)
ISBN: 978-0-9888547-7-2 (digital)

All rights reserved. No part of this book may be used or reproduced by any means, graphic, electronic, or mechanical, including photocopying, recording, taping or by any information storage retrieval system without the written permission of the publisher except in the case of brief quotations embodied in critical articles and reviews.

"Coconut," words and music by Harry Nilsson © 1972 (Renewed) Golden Syrup Music. All rights administered by Warner-Tamerlane Publishing Corp. All rights reserved. Used by permission.

Published in the United States of America by The Herby Lady, LLC

The author of this book does not dispense medical advice or prescribe the use of any technique as a form of treatment for physical, emotional, or medical problems without the advice of a physician, either directly or indirectly. The intent of the author is only to offer information of a general nature. In the event you use any of the information in this book for yourself, which is your constitutional right, the author and publisher assume no responsibility for your actions.

For all the kitchen witches…and witches in the kitchen.

Table of Contents

INTRODUCTION 1

ALFALFA 7

ALLSPICE 10

ALMOND 13

ALOE 16

ANGELICA 19

ANISE, ANISEED 22

APPLE 25

AVOCADO 29

BASIL (SWEET) 32

BAY, BAY LAUREL 36

BEET (WHITE AND RED) 39

BURDOCK 42

CALENDULA 45

CARAWAY 48

CARDAMOM 51

CATNIP, CATMINT 54

CAYENNE	57
CELERY	61
CHAMOMILE (GERMAN)	64
CILANTRO/CORIANDER	68
CINNAMON	71
CLOVE	74
CLOVER	77
COFFEE	80
DANDELION	83
DILL	86
ELDER	88
EUCALYPTUS	92
FENNEL	95
FENUGREEK	97
FLAX	100
GARLIC AND ONION	103
GINGER	107
HAWTHORN	111
HOPS	114

HOREHOUND	116
HYSSOP	119
IRISH MOSS	122
JASMINE	125
JUNIPER	127
LAVENDER	130
LEMON	133
LEMON BALM	137
LEMONGRASS	140
LIME	143
MARJORAM (SWEET)	145
MARSHMALLOW	147
MEADOWSWEET	150
MUGWORT	152
MUSTARD (BLACK/BROWN/WHITE)	155
NETTLE	158
NUTMEG	161
OLIVE	164
ORANGE	167

OREGANO	170
PARSLEY	173
PEPPER	176
PEPPERMINT	179
RICE	182
ROSE	185
ROSEMARY	189
RUE	193
SAGE	196
SPEARMINT	200
STAR ANISE	203
STRAWBERRY	205
TEA	208
THYME	212
YARROW	215
HONORABLE MENTION	219

INTRODUCTION

Everyone today wants more bang for their buck. We repurpose egg cartons as seed starters instead of purchasing something commercial; make plant food out of used coffee grounds and eggshells; or make a cup of tea to drink then use the bag to reduce puffy eyes. Saves the environment, saves money.

One place you *can* save money is your spice cupboard. A single herb can be used not only in tonight's dinner but to ease a headache or in a protection spell. Why have three when one will do? A majority of common herbs will do at least double, if not triple duty around the house.

In case you're new to using herbs, I'll give you a few pointers here:

If you can avoid it, *don't* buy your herbs or spices at the grocery store. Sure, they'll work just fine but you're paying through the nose. As an example, a jar of bay leaves at a local store costs around three dollars and weighs less than an ounce *including the plastic jar*. Conversely, you can get a full ounce of organic leaves in a ziplock bag off the Internet for around two dollars. Ask the cooks in your family to save their empty spice jars (you can put new labels on them), go in with a few friends (or those family cooks) on an order over the Internet, divvy it up when it arrives, and you'll all save *a lot of money*.

The three rules of dried herbs are no heat, no humidity and no light. The grocery store and even your health food store violate at least the last one by storing the herbs in clear containers exposed to a lot of light. Light slowly leaches the good stuff out of dried herbs. Moms all over the world violate the first and sometimes the second by keeping their spices in a cupboard close to the stove where they'll be handy for cooking. The heat from the stove and oven makes its way into that cupboard; the water they boil for pasta adds a lot of humidity to the air. Humidity allows mold and other fungi to flourish.

You however, are going to be proactive about keeping your herbs as fresh as possible for as long as possible. Yes, you'll want to keep some in a kitchen cupboard where they're easy to grab. But you're only going to keep an amount there that you'll use in three to four months. Everything else should be put in ziplock bags (squish all the air out before sealing) that are marked with the type of herb it is and the date you purchased it. These you'll put in a plastic tub (or at the very least a cardboard box) in the back of a closet away from any heat source. If one of your kitchen cupboards is on the other side of the room from the stove and hopefully on an outside wall so it stays cool most of the time, that's okay, too. Just ensure that wherever you store your box is as cool, dark and dry as you can make it. Replenish the kitchen supply from these bags as needed. Most properly-stored dried herbs will last about two years. Check them periodically. If they don't smell like they're supposed to, discard them (in a compost pile if possible) and get new stock.

Alternatively, if you do have a lot of shelf space (as in a large, walk-in pantry), store your herbs in half-pint or pint canning jars which you have coated with several layers of glass paint, then labeled. Those size of jars will hold an ounce or more of most herbs and the paint will keep light out.

Although it's not absolutely necessary, I'm going to advocate that you purchase an electric coffee grinder, even if you don't drink coffee. You can find a decent one for around ten dollars. My reason? First, using a mortar and pestle is *work*, and I'm lazy. Most of all, sometimes you'll want the whole herb while at others you'll want it ground. (Ground herbs make muddy teas.) Rather than buy both, you can grind just a little when your cake recipe calls for a teaspoon of ground whatever. Whole herbs keep longer than ground, since there's less surface area exposed to the air. As a bonus, fresh-ground is tastier – think of all the restaurants that give you the option of fresh-ground pepper on your meal. There's a reason they do that!

Before you add your herb to any liquid, crunch up the leaves or flowers in your hand; or smash the roots, bark or seeds with a hammer a few times. You want to open the pores so the liquid can leach out the chemical components. The surface pores close during the drying process and you want to expose the interior of your herb. You can use your grinder for this but don't grind them to a powder. The more finely ground your herb, the more difficult it is to strain.

Within this book I'll use the common word tea (small "t") for what's really either an infusion or a decoction of herbs. Tea (capital "T") is the herb *Camellia sinensis,* commonly referred to as black Tea or green Tea. To make an herbal infusion (for leaves and flowers), steep one teaspoon dried herb in one cup just-boiled water. Be sure to cover your cup: good stuff is in all that steam and you don't want it to escape. Ten minutes steeping time is a good rule of thumb. To make a decoction (for roots, barks and seeds), put one and one-third cups *cold* water in a pan with your teaspoon of dried herb and put it on the stove. Simmer (don't boil) until your liquid is reduced to a cup. In either case, strain the herb out before drinking or otherwise using.

I'll list the herbs alphabetically by the common name found on the jars in American grocery stores. I'll also give you the Latin binomial which is the "official" name of the plant. The Latin binomial is essential to know because common names can vary. You won't find the Latin binomial on any grocery store shelf but you *should* see them listed on a supplier's web page. If you don't, buy somewhere else. You want be certain what you're getting!

I'm not in any way suggesting you should obtain all sixty-nine herbs in this book. You'd need a whole closet, not a cupboard! However, based on your own needs, you can easily get away with twenty or thirty of them. I counted: I have twenty-seven, only five of which get used regularly. Rarely do I find a need to get an herb other than my regular stock and that's usually if I'm making up a specific preparation for another person.

Finally, I'm not going to include any recipes – cookery or otherwise. If I did, I would not only end up with a ten thousand page book (that in all honesty would never be finished), I'd certainly miss someone's favorite and hear about it. You can find a recipe for just about anything on the Internet. I'll give you suggestions and you do your own research. Deal?

ALFALFA

Medicago sativa

There's a reason farmers include alfalfa in their silage. (Silage: grass and/or other greens stored, typically in a silo, to feed cows and other livestock in winter. It generally ferments and smells wonderful.) Alfalfa is *very* high in various nutrients, notably vitamins C, E and K; and the minerals calcium, potassium, phosphorus and iron.

Parts Used The aerial (above-ground) part of the herb.

Cooking Can be used like virtually any other green: eat it raw, fry it or steam it. The sprouts are used similar to mung bean sprouts. Alfalfa sprouts are available in some grocery stores; I've never seen the leafy part. Alfalfa leaf powder is available commercially. You can sprinkle this on food. The dried leaf doesn't taste like much but it will add some vitamins to your dish. If you buy any part of it fresh, wash it thoroughly. Pesticide use on this crop is *very* common.

Medicinal Due to the high vitamin and mineral content, it's mostly used as a nutritive or tonic – good for helping those with appetite loss. It has a slight diuretic action so may be used in cases of water retention or in combination with other herbs to help kidney and bladder conditions. It is sometimes used in treatments for high cholesterol, diabetes and peptic ulcers. **Caution**: Excessive intake is not recommended. It can produce lupus-like symptoms or exacerbate systemic lupus erythematosus (SLE). It also may have estrogenic effects on some people. Eating it as a side dish or adding some sprouts to your sandwich once or twice a week shouldn't pose a problem (if you don't have SLE) but if you take it in supplement form, follow the instructions carefully.

Magical This is where alfalfa really shines. Because of the nutritive action, use it in anti-hunger spells. Alfalfa is "rich" in vitamins and minerals so incorporate it into spells for prosperity or money. Keep a small jar of it in your cupboard or pantry to ward off hunger.

Grow It Yourself Seeds are definitely available! It's not only used as a livestock crop but also as a cover crop to prevent erosion or to enrich poor soil. You probably won't get much out of a pot of alfalfa growing in a sunny windowsill but if you have a small space outside, plant it in spring, at about ½" depth. It tolerates most any type of soil. Harvest it before it blooms.

Notes

ALLSPICE

Pimenta dioica

What we know as "allspice" is the dried fruit of an evergreen tree native to Mexico and Central America. It's said the English coined the name in the early 1600s because it tastes like a combination of cinnamon, nutmeg and cloves. While it may be called "pimento" by some, what we know as pimento here in the United States is actually a sweet cherry pepper.

Parts Used Fruit.

Cooking Add two or three dried fruits to mulled wine or cider (a little goes a long way). It's an ingredient in Jamaican Jerked Chicken as well as other dishes from the Caribbean, Mexico and some parts of Indonesia (where it is now cultivated). It can be ground with black pepper and used as a finish for baked meats.

Medicinal Makes an excellent addition to preparations that normally wouldn't taste very good. Because it's strong tasting and smelling, a pinch in a cup of tea is all that's needed. A small amount per day (one or two teaspoons of the whole fruit) will help with dyspepsia or flatulence. Topically, like cloves, it can be an anesthetic.

Magical Used mostly in luck and money spells, but it can also be added to healing work or to add a little boost to nearly any magical undertaking. It definitely makes a lovely-smelling incense. According to Judika Illes' *The Element Encyclopedia of 5000 Spells*, the fruits should be strung and worn as a necklace to enhance a business venture. I hope you have strong fingers. The dried fruit is *hard*. Allspice is also said to be helpful in spells to turn around bad investments.

Grow It Yourself Seeds are available or if you live in a tropical climate and have access to them, you can extract the two seeds from fresh fruit. Ensure the seeds are fresh as well. They lose their viability after only two short months. Allspice will grow outdoors in USDA zones 10-11, although you may be able to grow it in a sheltered spot in zone 9. Otherwise, it's a houseplant. The seeds need to be kept very warm and moist and can take up to three months to germinate. If you're lucky, you'll end up with an evergreen shrub.

Notes

ALMOND

Prunus amygdalus var. dulcis

Here I will write of the *sweet* almond (the *var. dulcis* part of the above name). There is also *bitter* almond, which is the original, wild almond. Bitter almond contains prussic acid, which turns into cyanide when eaten. The sweet almond is a mutation of its wild brother and is thought to be one of the first trees to be domesticated. It does not contain prussic acid.

Parts Used Oil, seed.

Cooking You don't have to add them to anything – eat as they are! But if you want to, many main and side dishes contain almonds; almond milk is used as a substitute for cow's milk; almond butter is just as good as peanut butter; marzipan, that tasty holiday treat, is a thick almond paste; and according to *The Huffington Post*, the chocolate industry uses 40% of the world's supply of almonds.

Medicinal Almond oil is very light yet a good emollient so it makes a great base oil for ointments and creams. It also doesn't have a strong odor so it won't overpower the aroma of other herbs or essential oils. Eating almonds as part of a healthy lifestyle may help reduce cholesterol and control diabetes. In India, almonds were traditionally given to nursing mothers and invalids to help boost the immune system and provide general nutritional support. **Caution**: In large doses, ingestion of the oil is toxic, causing depression of the central nervous system and respiratory failure.

Magical Almonds are a seed and like almost any other seed, useful in workings for prosperity and money. Perhaps a subcontinent version of the Druids' hazelnut, almonds are said to be helpful in workings for wisdom, or to overcome dependency or addiction.

Grow It Yourself Although a small tree, it is nonetheless a *tree* and wants room. Therefore, it needs to be outside, in USDA zones 6 and higher. Plant a fresh, unprocessed nut covered with two or three inches of soil in late fall. In the appropriate zones, you may be able to find seedlings at a garden center. If you only want to plant one tree, ensure you get one that is self-pollinating. Many cultivars aren't. Be patient – it'll take five years or more before you'll get blooms and then nuts.

Notes

ALOE

Aloe vera, Aloe barbadensis

Everyone knows this herb, or at least the gel as a great method of burn relief, right? There's so much more to it than that.

Parts Used Leaf, gel.

Cooking The leaves are popular in Asian and Latin American cuisine. They do require some preparation: the gel needs to be allowed to drip out (save it!), the skin of the leaf needs to be peeled off, and only the flesh cooked. They can be simmered alone with your favorite spices from those areas of the world or added to stews and soups like any other vegetable. Boil the cubed flesh in sugar water for a sweet treat.

Medicinal As noted above, slathering the gel on a burn will provide nearly instant cooling. It will also quickly take the sting out of insect bites. It's frequently used in combination with other herbs and/or oils for treatment of acne, eczema, psoriasis and thinning hair. Aloe gel will assist with wound healing *but* may slow the process down a bit, especially in deep "wounds" such as surgical incisions. The juice is drunk to help with ulcers or as a laxative. **Caution:** Do not ingest during pregnancy or lactation; with any intestinal obstruction or abdominal pain of unknown origin; hemorrhoids; or kidney dysfunction. Should not be used internally by children younger than 12 or for more than eight to ten days.

Magical Thought to bring luck and protection. Having a growing plant in the house will provide protection (especially from household accidents). In Latin America, a leaf is hung over the door to attract luck and provide protection to those who reside within. If you have any concerns when doing magical workings, put a live plant on your altar to protect you from dangerous spirits.

Grow It Yourself Aloe is a succulent, just like cacti, so it prefers a warm, dry environment. Unless you live in the desert, plan on keeping it as a houseplant. In the wild, it will grow two to three feet tall but as a potted plant, you'll probably see a foot at most. Mature plants can be found at most garden centers. Put it in a sunny window, watering it only when the soil is very dry. Watch for spider mites, aphids and the like as they will literally suck the life out of your plant.

A mature plant will produce "pups," which can be divided off and repotted to grow on their own.

Notes

ANGELICA

Angelica archangelica

How sweet it is! Did you know Angelica is one of the ingredients in booze? Liqueurs and aquavits to be exact. Check out Chartreuse, Bénédictine, vermouth, and Dubonnet. You can find the fruits (mericarps) in recipes for absinthe, as well. Music is sweet, too. The hollow stem can be used to make a type of flute.

Parts Used Leaves, root, stem.

Cooking Angelica stems are candied and used as cake decorations (or eaten alone…). However, the leaves are used to flavor fish or in salads; the stalk can be cooked with apples or rhubarb when making crumbles or made into a jam.

Medicinal The root is not only the most aromatic part of the plant, it's the part most used in medicine. A tea or tincture may be helpful in cases of bronchitis, colds, flu, pleurisy or flatulence. Because it's sweetish, it may induce those with appetite loss to eat. **Caution**: May interfere with anticoagulant therapies. May cause photosensitivity reactions in sensitive individuals.

Magical Considered one of the most powerful herbs for protection – attracts positive energy and repels negative. Life got you down? Make a tea of angelica (any part of the plant), drink it and/or add it to bath water to raise your spirits. Useful in healing and uncrossing work. If you work with the archangel Michael, offer this to him. It's said it got the "archangelica" part of its name because Michael was the one who suggested this plant was medicine.

Grow It Yourself You can. In the garden or in a *very* large pot on your deck or patio. Angelica has a very long taproot so you want enough depth for it. Plant it in a semi-shady to sunny location and keep it damp. It won't look like much the first year – just a rosette of leaves with a stalk maybe a foot or so tall. The second year it will shoot up to six feet tall with beautiful umbels of white flowers. After that second year, the plant may die. It's considered either a biennial or a very short-lived perennial. Be sure to save some of the seeds that will hang off the flowers so you can plant them. **Caution**: Angelica does grow in the wild in the northern hemisphere but *be sure of what you're harvesting.* It looks very similar to poisonous genera such as *Conium* and *Heracleum*.

Notes

ANISE, ANISEED
Pimpinella anisum

I seem to have alcohol on the brain: Anise is the flavoring in ouzo. It may be an acquired taste for many but ouzo is nearly considered the national drink of Greece. It's so popular in that country there are *ouzeries*…bars that specialize in ouzo. In 2006 the Greek government won the exclusive rights to the name "ouzo". Sambuca, a popular Italian liqueur, is also anise-flavored. This is typically served with three whole coffee beans, symbolizing health, happiness and prosperity. There's also anisette…

Parts Used Seed.

Cooking Because it has a licorice-type flavor, it's mostly used in baking (and booze). Commercial "licorice" sweets now generally use anise as their flavoring. Anise can be found in many cultures' seasoning blends for chicken, pork, curry and sausage. **Note:** Star anise (*Illicium verum*), while not even related to true anise, may be substituted in cooking. They taste almost identical.

Medicinal Anise is antispasmodic and an expectorant, making it useful for coughs associated with bronchitis, colds and pertussis (whooping cough). If you don't have fennel around (another licorice-y herb), use anise for flatulence. **Caution**: May interfere with anticoagulant therapies. May cause allergic reactions and photosensitivity.

Magical Whole seeds placed in a dream pillow will help ward off nightmares. Also useful to ward off the evil eye, find happiness and stimulate psychic activity. While used in spells to attract love, it's best to use this when working on *yourself* rather than drawing someone to you. If you need extra strength in spells using anise, use one of the anise-flavored liqueurs listed above rather than anise tea.

Grow It Yourself Anise is an annual so you should be able to grow it just about anywhere. It has a long taproot so you'll want to ensure your garden plot or patio pot has enough depth for it. It does not like to be moved so plant it in its final spot or transplant seedlings only. It likes warmth so sow when the soil is warm, in full sun and light soil. Give it moderate moisture. Aniseed isn't really a seed at all but the fruit of the plant.

Notes

APPLE

Malus domestica; syn. *Pyrus malus*

There are over 7,500 cultivars of this ubiquitous plant. Cultivated since probably before recorded history, it is found in Greek mythology, the Norse Edda, as well as various interpretations of the Bible.

Parts Used Fruit.

Cooking Given the number of cultivars, you want to be sure you have the correct *type* of apple for your dish. Do you want tart (Granny Smith)? Sweet (Honeycrisp)? Are you going to eat it alone, put it in a salad, bake it? All these factors must be considered for the perfect eating experience. Some examples of apple uses include ciders (hard and soft); butters; chutneys; cakes; turnovers; pies; salads; as a garnish or included in pork dishes; or baked alone.

Medicinal Apples are very healthy eating. A recent research study found that people who ate an apple 15 minutes before lunch ate almost 190 fewer calories than those who didn't. Makes sense. The high fiber content in an apple (not to mention the acidic content) would make you feel somewhat full prior to picking up your fork.

But it's not just that. The pectin encourages the growth of beneficial bacteria in the digestive tract and may reduce high cholesterol and high blood pressure. Apples are full of flavonoids, which are antioxidants. These help improve immune system function. One of those flavonoids, quercetin, may kill the herpes virus that causes cold sores.

Green apples help cleanse the liver and gallbladder (again, the acidic content); eating an apple gives your gums a nice massage and helps to clean your teeth at the same time. Be sure to leave the peel on. This helps with the massage and most of the healthful chemical compounds are located just below the peel.

Caution: Crushing the seed releases a form of cyanide. The few seeds found in one apple probably won't hurt you, but crunching on a lot of them may make you nauseated or give you a headache. In *large* quantities, cyanide poisoning can lead to respiratory failure and death.

Magical From a magical perspective, how and why apples and love became associated with each other isn't terribly clear. Perhaps it's because in the 7th century BCE, apples were so expensive in Attica, Greece, that bridal couples had to share one on their wedding night. However, it must go further back than that. Apples are a favorite of the goddess Aphrodite, the Greek goddess of love. I'm pretty sure she was around long before the 7th century!

Whatever, the apple is now used in spells designed to divine love. One that I remember from my youth: as you peel an apple, recite the alphabet. When the peel either breaks or is completely removed, the letter you're on will be the first letter of the first name of your "true love." I'm not sure this spell works… My grandmother was a whiz at peeling an apple in one continuous spiral and my grandfather's name started with 'A.' I, on the other hand, after all these years of making pie, still can't manage more than a turn or two before the peel breaks and my beloved's name starts with a 'P.'

The apple is strongly associated with Samhain. Even the mundane Halloween celebrations bob for apples. It's said the apple symbolizes the dead and in some celebrations is burned in honor of those who will be reborn in the spring.

Other uses include spells for healing, immortality and banishment.

Grow It Yourself If you have a lot of room on your property and a *lot* of time, you, too, can have an apple orchard. Apples generally like USDA zones 3 to 8 but check with your local nursery for the best cultivar for your area. They do not self-pollinate so you will need more than one tree. They are also very susceptible to fungus, bugs and bacterial infections, and growing them organically requires careful watching and patience. Owning an apple orchard is not for the faint of heart!

Notes

AVOCADO

Persea americana

This fruit has been around as long as the apple, albeit in a different part of the world. It's thought to be native to Mexico and Central America. According to Wikipedia, evidence of avocado use has been found in a cave in Mexico, dating to about 10,000 BCE. The etymology of the common name is interesting: a corruption of Spanish into English rather than the green, lumpy skin gave us the nickname "Alligator Pear".

Parts Used Fruit, leaves, bark.

Cooking Unless you live under a rock, you know the most popular use for avocado is in guacamole. They can also be baked or roasted and served alone as a side dish, or as part of a salad or sandwich. One site I looked at suggested shirring eggs in the depression left after the pit has been removed. The avocado can be found in dishes of cultures throughout the world, including parts of Asia and Africa where it can be found in sweet drinks, including milkshakes.

Also like the apple, there are myriad cultivars, some good for cooking, some not.

Medicinal If you have access to the tree, a decoction of the fresh leaves or bark will help with diarrhea. If all you have is the fruit you purchased at the store, mash it and use it as a poultice to help heal wounds, or use it as a facial mask to help draw out blemishes. The oil (pressed from the fruit) is also nourishing to the skin. Although a high-fat fruit, the fat is mono-unsaturated which makes it a good addition to the diet of people with high cholesterol.

Magical Like the apple, avocado is used in love, lust and sex magic. If you grow your own tree (see below), pick the first fruit from that tree, eat it and carry the cleaned and dried pit as a love charm. Probably due to the high fat content that makes it wonderful for skin preparations, it's also used in beauty spells.

Grow It Yourself It's a school science experiment! Take the pit of a fruit that has not been refrigerated, stab three or four toothpicks into it about a third of the way up from the round bottom, suspend it in a glass of tepid water and wait. In four to six weeks, the bottom should split and roots should start growing out of it. (If it doesn't grow roots, throw that one out and start over.) You can then transplant it into a pot. It may not be attractive but given time, you'll have a tree. In four to six years, your tree will bear fruit. Similar to bananas, avocados ripen off the tree. Pick the fruit when it's still hard and allow it to ripen in a cool spot.

Notes

BASIL (SWEET)
Ocimum basilicum

I know a lot of cooks who have a basil plant in a pot on the windowsill in their kitchen. They swear it's better fresh than dried. (It really is but if all you have is dried, go for it.) If you have a sunny windowsill (and, unlike me, no cats to bother it), go ahead and get a plant at the local nursery. Be aware that although it's considered perennial (lives a long time), it's a picky plant and yours may not last beyond a year. If you really want fresh basil but can't keep a plant, buy it in the produce section of your grocery store, strip the leaves from the stems, place them on a cookie sheet and put them in the freezer for a few hours. Store the frozen leaves in a ziplock bag in your freezer, using as necessary – they'll thaw quickly in cooking.

Watch your labels: Thai basil, while its Latin binomial is indeed *O. basilicum*, is a cultivar. That means it's been bred to taste the way it does. You'll usually find Thai basil listed as *O. basilicum var. Horapha*. I understand it's more licorice-y than common basil.

Parts Used Aerial.

Cooking Commonly found in Mediterranean and Asian dishes. Goes well with tomatoes, mild cheeses and pork. It's an ingredient in pesto. Add a few leaves to your grilled zucchini, corn or shrimp. Use as a garnish on tomato or squash soup. Always add basil at the last minute: cooking destroys its flavor and adding it early will give you a hay-like taste.

While we westerners normally use only the leaves or above-ground parts of the plant, in Asia, the seeds are soaked in water, become gelatinous and are used in drinks and desserts.

Medicinal A tea can be used externally as a wash to combat acne or to treat warts (which are caused by a virus). Drinking that same tea can help with colds, flu, sore throat and coughs; help with stomach cramps and flatulence; and as a diuretic, may help with some kidney problems and fluid retention. Some women use the tea before and after childbirth to promote blood circulation and help with milk flow.

Magical The most widely-known use for basil is in money spells. Carry a leaf in your wallet. If you have your own business (or really like the one you work for), place that leaf in the cash register or use a tea as a wash – especially around the door.

Basil will confer protection to a person (carry the leaves on you) or a home (anoint the doors and windows with either the essential oil or a wash). Do the same to drive off negative energy and repair your protection shield.

My favorite: give the gift of a basil plant to someone moving into a new home. It confers protection on the house, brings luck and is useful in the kitchen. The plant owner should then gift a leaf to each guest as they're leaving the house to ensure a safe journey home.

Grow It Yourself As stated above, many people have a fresh plant on their kitchen windowsill. Basil will grow from seed in a pot or in the garden but you have to watch it carefully: it will bolt easily (produce flowers) and this is detrimental to the taste. Pinch off every flower bud you see. This will prevent it from re-seeding itself and when the plant dies, you'll have to either get a new one from the nursery or start from scratch with purchased seeds.

Notes

BAY, BAY LAUREL
Laurus nobilis

You'll almost always find bay leaves dried. As a matter of fact, I don't think I've ever seen them fresh. At least not on my side of the pond in my climate zone. I know the shrub is hardy to zone 8, so it's probably found in my vacation spots but I haven't noticed it.

Parts Used Leaves.

Cooking Common in Cuban and French cuisine (bay is one of the ingredients in a *bouquet garni*), it goes well in soups (especially bean or lentil), stews and marinades. A couple of leaves are added to a traditional corned beef and cabbage dish. It's used as a flavoring when braising meats (especially beef). I put a couple in my pot of chili. Bay leaves are usually used whole and then removed before serving – the leaves are leathery and sharp, which doesn't make for a pleasant dining experience.

Medicinal Bay tea is a good diaphoretic – it makes you sweat. It's helpful for fevers in this regard. Use that same tea as an after-shampoo rinse to help get rid of dandruff. An ointment is used externally as a rub to soothe arthritis pains. You can also use the diluted essential oil for dandruff and rheumatism/arthritis rubs.

Bay is also sometimes used alone or part of a mixture as an insect repellant. **Caution:** Some people may find bay to be a skin irritant. Do a patch test before using.

Magical Drink a cup of tea before any divination activity to strengthen your powers or place a leaf under your pillow for prophetic dreams.

To use as a divination tool: write your wish on a bay leaf and then set fire to the leaf. If it burns, chances are your wish will come true. If it won't light or the flame sputters and dies, you may want to reconsider your wish.

If you suspect poltergeist activity in your home, burn bay during your exorcism then hang a few leaves up around the house in the corners of rooms to discourage their return and provide protection for the inhabitants.

A sprig of bay can be used to sprinkle water or washes during purification ceremonies.

It's useful in nearly any healing or purification spell.

Grow It Yourself Bay is hardy outdoors in USDA zones 8 to 10 but will grow happily in a pot in the house. *Watch your plant name.* There are several plants that have the common name "bay" and not all of them are useful in cookery or medicine.

Bay can be started from seed but it's very slow to germinate – it may take six months or more before you see a sprout. Most nurseries carry seedlings. Although it will grow as tall as sixty feet, it will be a small tree in a pot, or can be pruned to shrub-height outdoors. Soil isn't that important but watering is. The roots tend to stay shallow so don't let the soil dry out.

Notes

BEET (WHITE AND RED)
Beta vulgaris

Perhaps not the prettiest of herbs/vegetables but useful nonetheless. Beet is a root vegetable so you may find it listed as "beetroot". We're still talking about the same plant.

Parts Used Root, leaves (in cookery).

Cooking As a root vegetable, it can be prepared like just about any other: roasting, boiling, and canning. It's probably most famous as the prime ingredient in borscht, a soup that has made its way farther into the world from the Slavic countries. Borscht (and other beet-based soups) can be served either hot or cold. Pickled beets can be eaten on their own or as a part of salads. Beets are sweet and are made into a sugar just like cane sugar. The leaves can be cooked just as any other green and are higher in several minerals (including iron) than spinach, turnip or mustard greens.

Medicinal Beets have been the subject of much research in recent years. Some sources say drinking one glass of (red) beet juice each day will lower systolic blood pressure by as much as five points. The same juice can provide a boost to stamina and the immune system and can be part of a diet in the treatment of cancer. The greens are high in lutein and zeaxanthin, which are compounds essential to eye health. White beet supports the liver and gallbladder. A decoction of both leaf and root used as a rinse will help with dandruff. **Caution:** Some people may experience reddening of the urine when eating beets in normal amounts. For most people it's not an issue but it *could* be indicative of a problem metabolizing iron.

Magical Beets are associated with attracting love. It's said if a man and woman eat the same beet, they will fall in love. Use the juice as ink in written spells or, for the squeamish, as a blood substitute.

Grow It Yourself Beets like cool weather so those in temperate climates may want to plant them in the fall for winter/spring harvest. They will even survive frost and some freezing temperatures but don't like anything above 75° F. They like partial to full sun and a well-drained, neutral pH soil. Keep them moist, during both germination and growing. Most varieties will mature in 50 to 70 days.

Notes

BURDOCK

Arctium lappa

Burdock flowers are prickly and will stick to anything. They are the inspiration for Velcro®!

Parts Used Leaves, root, seed.

Cooking The root, while tough, will soften when cooked. It is roasted, sautéed, boiled, however you like to prepare root vegetables. It can be sliced and deep-fried like potato chips and is healthier for you. Burdock is an ingredient in a traditional Japanese dish called, "kinpira gobo," which, from all accounts, looks like a vegetable side dish. The leaves are large enough to use as a wrap when cooking over an open fire, similar to grape leaves.

Medicinal Burdock's list of therapeutic actions contains a lot of "anti" words. Antibacterial, antibiotic, anti-inflammatory... Use it externally for acne, cradle cap, dandruff, eczema, psoriasis and wound-healing. A *mild* decoction of the root (half-strength) may be taken internally to help clear skin issues. An infusion of the leaves will help with digestive issues and is considered to be a blood purifier/tonic as well. Recent studies suggest the root (eaten as a vegetable) contains prebiotic properties, which also help with digestive problems. Its high nutritional value makes the root valuable in treating anorexia. **Caution:** May interfere with hypoglycemic therapies.

Magical Useful in protection spells: can be carried, strewn around the home or used in incenses for such. Wards off or cleanses acquired negativity, especially if you're feeling down about yourself (add a decoction of the root to your bath water). It will add a boost to any healing spell. It's said that placing the leaves in shoes will heal gout. Although not a traditional meaning, I find the flower heads useful to make something "stick" to me, e.g., money (so I don't spend it).

Grow It Yourself Burdock is a biennial, meaning it only lasts two years. And it's *tall*. Plants may grow to six feet in height or more. Sow seeds in a light soil and keep moist but not wet. It doesn't require full sun and will tolerate partial shade. Only leaves will appear the first year; the second will see your plants shoot up and produce flowers, which turn into those sticky seed heads. Although your plant will die after that second year, it readily re-seeds itself and can become a nuisance around other plants.

Notes

CALENDULA

Calendula officinalis

This bright plant is otherwise known as "pot marigold". Not only because it grows in pots (it will) but because the flowers can be used as a potherb – in cookery. It's also not your mother's *marigold*. While pretty, "regular" marigolds are of the *Tagetes* genus.

Parts Used Flowers.

Cooking The petals (pulled off the bitter flower center) are used in fish and meat soups, rice dishes and salads. The petals are rather chewy, even when cooked, so it might be best to chop them first. It's said that in the 1600s, grocers carried calendula by the barrel-full because the Dutch used it extensively in winter broths. The leaves have been used as "greens" but they are rather bitter.

Medicinal It is anti-inflammatory, astringent and antimicrobial, and is great for healing wounds, cuts, scrapes, rashes, bee stings, burns and bruises. It is mild enough that it can be used on babies (to heal diaper rash) and is now extensively used in creams for stretch marks. Because of its anti-inflammatory and antimicrobial properties, a gargle of calendula extract can be used for sores in the mouth and other inflammations of the mouth and throat. It also contains large amounts of iodine, manganese and carotene, all of which help regenerate skin cells. However, because it does regenerate skin quickly, you never want to use it when there's infection present. It will heal the skin over the infection. **Caution:** Calendula is a member of the *Asteraceae* family, just like ragweed, and may cause similar reactions.

Magical Calendula is wonderful in protection spells and those for legal matters and psychic powers. A garland of flowers on your door will prevent evil from entering; scatter those flowers under your bed for nightly protection and to make dreams come true. Carry a flower or two in your pocket to put you in a favorable light with the judge. You may want to try the same thing when going to a job interview – to have the interviewer smile favorably upon you. Make an infused oil or an infusion with the flowers and use it to consecrate tools. The bright yellow flowers will help if you're invoking the Sun in any spell, too.

Grow It Yourself Calendula isn't a picky plant ... it *will* grow easily in a pot but be aware that there is only one flower per stem, so you won't get many. You can start it from seed indoors or sow directly into the soil after the last frost. It likes full sun but in very hot climates, you might want to put it in partial shade. It is a perennial plant but I've found it only lasts about three years before I need to re-seed that bed. If you pick the blooms when they're at their fullest, most plants will bloom from late spring to early fall. (Warning: I had read that rabbits didn't like it. Apparently our neighborhood rabbits didn't get the message. Ours love it.) The same seed packet will yield flowers anywhere from a bright, sunny yellow to a deep orange. The deeper the orange, the more medicinally potent the flower.

Notes

CARAWAY
Carum carvi

This member of the carrot family has soft, fern-like leaves, similar to fennel, and has a similar, licorice-y aroma. What we think of as "seeds" are actually the fruit of the caraway plant. You may be surprised to find it as a fragrance in your favorite cosmetics, perfumes or soaps.

Parts Used Mostly seed but leaves and root in cookery.

Cooking Caraway is what gives rye bread its distinctive flavor. It pairs well with garlic but not usually other spices. It can be found in German and Austrian dishes such as sauerkraut and the Danish Havarti cheese. Put a pinch in potato salad or cole slaw; add it to fish, pork and Polish sausage dishes. It's the headliner in British caraway cakes and Middle Eastern caraway pudding, usually served at Ramadan. It's an ingredient in Akvavit and other liqueurs. The leaves are used as a green similar to parsley and the root can be cooked like turnips.

Medicinal The seeds can be chewed as a breath freshener. It is useful for digestive problems such as gas, bloating and intestinal cramps. It may be an appetite stimulant. The oil (pressed from the fruit) is used by women to bring on menstruation and some nursing mothers use it to help the flow of milk. As an expectorant, it can help expel phlegm from the lungs during bronchitis.

Magical Want to prevent a lover from straying? Serve him/her the aforementioned British caraway cakes or another sweet with the seeds as an ingredient. Depending on how you word your spell, the same cakes can be simply lust-inducing. Put some seeds on/in/around an object you want to make theft-proof. A small bag of seeds placed in a child's crib will prevent illness, or put that bag under your pillow to strengthen your memory and help you remember your dreams. Use a decoction of the seeds to consecrate a tool and prevent it from "growing legs" (leaving your house).

Grow It Yourself While not a common garden plant, it will grow in an indoor pot or outdoors in cooler climates. It is slow to germinate and dislikes being overwatered. The foliage is very susceptible to rot if kept wet. It is a biennial: only leaves and a short stalk will emerge the first year. (Being a relative of the carrot, it has a long taproot. Be sure your pot or bed is deep enough to accommodate it.) The second year will see it grow to two feet or so tall, and small white flowers will appear before the fruit (seed).

Notes

CARDAMOM

Elettaria cardamomum

This relative of ginger may be either of the genus *Elettaria* (green or true cardamom) or *Amomum* (black, brown or red cardamom). Either will work and both are native to the Indian peninsula, although they're now cultivated in other, temperate climates. It is the world's third-most expensive spice, right behind saffron and vanilla.

Parts Used Seed.

Cooking Cardamom is a frequent ingredient in curries so it's useful in any Indian-inspired dish, most frequently in rice or roasted meat preparations. In cooking, you'll need to distinguish between the two genera: true cardamom is somewhat minty while the black/brown/red variety has a hot-spicy flavor, similar to its cousin, ginger. In Scandinavian countries, cardamom is used frequently in place of cinnamon.

Medicinal Like its cousin, cardamom is aromatic, making it good for clearing congested bronchial passages (bronchitis or asthma). An infusion of the seeds or a few drops of tincture can help with indigestion and gastritis. The essential oil, diluted in a carrier oil, may be massaged on the abdomen to help with digestive pain, or onto a muscle cramp to help it relax.

Magical The seeds are added to sachets to attract love or just induce lust. Infusing the seeds into wine may achieve the same thing. If you need to charm someone (either a love/lust interest or an audience if you're giving a lecture), chew a few seeds beforehand. Cardamom also helps provide clarity so may be used prior to any divination activity.

Grow It Yourself A native of tropical forests, cardamom does not do well outdoors in most climates. It refuses to grow if temperatures fall below 63° F. You can grow it as a houseplant, though, provided you are able to give it enough humidity. It is generally propagated from fresh seed or rhizome division. It will tolerate most any soil and prefers mostly shade with only indirect sunlight, just as it would get in its native home. It will grow into a large shrub or small tree in ideal circumstances and has a lifespan of 10-15 years.

Notes

CATNIP, CATMINT
Nepeta cataria

Who doesn't know catnip? Even if you're not a cat lover, you know of the effect it has on *most* cats. (I say most because I've had cats that completely ignored it in favor of other herbs.) It can be tough to grow in a garden…not because it's a difficult plant to grow but because you'll attract every stray or outdoor cat in the neighborhood who will chew on it, roll in it, trample on it…

Parts Used Leaf.

Cooking This was a tough one! At first, I couldn't find any mention of catnip in cuisine other than the occasional cup of tea. Some of my friends suggested using it in recipes that called for basil – another very aromatic plant. However, I was diligent and found mention of it added as another green to salads, as an ingredient in meat marinades, or wherever you find a need for a strong-smelling member of the mint family, perhaps in pesto. I even found a recipe for catnip cookies.

Medicinal Catnip is mild and doesn't taste bad at all, so you can give a child a cup of tea for an upset tummy or about a half hour before bed to help the little one sleep. (Or should I say, help Mom and Dad sleep?) The calming effect helps hiccups better than a glass of plain water. It is antipyretic, a refrigerant, and diaphoretic so will assist in bringing down a fever. If I'm out of lemon balm, a cup of catnip tea is my next-favorite to ease a tension headache.

Magical Catnip is, *for some odd reason*, sacred to Bast. Therefore, use it in any spell involving her, other cat deities, or cats in general. Bast is a warrior goddess (she originally had a lion's head, not that of a domestic cat) and it's said that chewing the leaves will confer courage, fierceness and protection.

Catnip is used, in conjunction with rose petals, in spells for attracting love. As well, add it to spells for enhancing beauty or promoting happiness. Mix it with dragon's blood and burn to rid oneself of a bad habit or other behavior problem.

Grow It Yourself Catnip, like almost any other member of the mint family, is quite easy to grow from seed. Sow seeds outdoors after the last frost in a mostly-sunny area of your garden. It doesn't require any special soil or watering, although augmenting sandy or clayey soil will produce a stronger plant. Also like most mints, it will take over an area so give it plenty of room. It is a hardy perennial and will survive most northern winters.

Notes

CAYENNE

Capsicum annuum

The genus *Capsicum* encompasses not only the fruits we know as chili peppers but also the more benign bell peppers. It is the cultivar that determines no heat, hot, hotter and hottest. The Scoville scale is used to determine the "heat factor": zero being a bell pepper (which has had the capsaicin bred out of it) all the way to the 2,200,000 Scoville Heat Units of the "Carolina Reaper." The ubiquitous jalapeños range from 1,000 to 4,000 and habaneros 100,000 and up. Most pepper spray sold is about 500,000 units but it depends on the dilution.

Capsicums are natives of North and South America. The story goes that Columbus brought it back to Europe as a substitute for the very-expensive black pepper.

To confuse things even further, the spice paprika is also made from *C. annuum*. Unlike cayenne powder (which is made from the whole fruit including the seeds), paprika is made from just the meat of the fruit alone.

Parts Used Fruit.

Cooking Pick your heat! Most Mexican/Tex-Mex restaurants will serve jalapeños as a garnish on virtually every dish. Fresh red or green cayenne peppers can be used in a similar fashion, as can the hotter habaneros. The peppers can be chopped and added to dips, sauces, soups and main courses. Cayenne has been added to hot chocolate, beef stew, curries and roasted nuts. For less heat, remove the seeds and white inner flesh before using. This won't kill all the heat, just some.

The milder bell peppers are stuffed; may be sliced and eaten raw, sautéed or roasted and are added to anything from salads to pizza to soups.

NB: Most people reach for water or another cold drink when the heat from a pepper gets to them. This will only exacerbate the pain, as it dilutes and spreads the capsaicin around the mouth. Drink whole milk or eat yogurt or sour cream instead. In a pinch, pop a pat of butter into your mouth. The fat molecules in dairy bind with the capsaicin and take it away from the nerve receptors.

Medicinal Capsicum ointment is widely used topically for muscle strains, sprains and cramps. Its efficacy is so well-known, you can even buy it commercially. (Be careful. The beautiful red that signals warmth will also stain your clothing.) Less-known but becoming more so is the fact that it can help with indigestion, laryngitis, sore throats and I've even heard that a pinch of powder on the tip of the tongue will help a migraine headache. This is one of the times that if you choose to use an infusion, you want to dilute it yet again. To use internally, make a standard infusion then put a tablespoon of *that* in a cup of water before drinking. **Caution**: While it can help clear up diarrhea, excessive doses can *cause* diarrhea. Sensitive individuals may experience nausea, too. *Do not use on mucous membranes.*

Magical Do you need to "heat up" a situation? I don't necessarily mean in the love department, although there's that. How about "lighting a fire" under someone to get them moving in your preferred direction? Adding cayenne powder or the dried, chopped fruit can help here. (If you choose to add it to incense, don't breathe in the fumes!) Scatter the powder around the house to break hexes or curses and as a prophylactic – it will repel negative energy. It will speed up the effect of any spell.

Grow It Yourself Although the species name, *annuum*, implies that capsicum is an annual, it really isn't. As long as they don't get frost-bitten, the shrubs will survive year after year. Most everything you read about growing tomatoes or bell peppers will apply to capsicum. They are, after all, relatives. Due to time-to-fruit (up to 150 days after you see the first leaves for some of the hotter varieties), most people in less-than-temperate climates start their plants indoors in January or February. Outdoors, plant seeds after the last frost in a sunny location. The soil should be slightly sandy so it drains well. Peppers like a lot of moisture but not so much their roots get waterlogged. Do not overfeed. Doing so will produce lush leaves but few to no fruit.

Notes

CELERY

Apium graveolens

When considering celery, most people think of the green stalks found in the produce aisle at the store. Here, however, we're concerned with the seed, a seed so small it looks as if it's already been ground.

Parts Used Seed.

Cooking The stalks may be slightly sweet but the seed has a warm, yet bitter flavor. Use it in soup stocks, the water you boil your shellfish in, mayonnaise, homemade pickles, potato salad, in a rub for grilled meats or put a pinch in your meatloaf. My recipe for cocktail sauce includes celery seed. Some people don't like the bitter taste and will grind celery seed to a powder before use. This will remove some of the acridity.

Medicinal Perhaps to counteract the almost 95% water content of the stalks, the seeds are diuretic, making them useful in combination with other herbs to treat a urinary tract infection or to help with water weight gain. They are slightly anti-inflammatory and anti-spasmodic so may be included in arthritis preparations. **Caution:** May provoke a photo-sensitive reaction in some people.

Magical Chewing the seeds will help strengthen mental powers, making them useful prior to any divination activity or before studying for an exam. Or add them to any incense prepared for such activity. Adding them to a dream pillow will induce sleep. Like most any other seed, they are associated with fertility. If you can find a whole stalk with the seeds still attached, eating that stalk supposedly induces lust.

Grow It Yourself If you've purchased a whole bunch of celery at the store, don't throw away the base after you've cut the stalks off! Instead, place the base (base down, stalks up) in a saucer of water in a sunny windowsill. Change the water every couple of days. After a week or so, you'll find that the outside stalks dry up but in the center, little yellow leaves will appear. After you see those leaves, transfer the base to a pot full of rich potting soil (or outdoors if it's warm enough), covering everything except the leaves. Water generously & mist frequently. You should be able to start harvesting fresh celery in a few months.

If all you have are seeds, you're in for a challenge. Celery is *very* slow to germinate and likes temperatures above 70° F to do so. Because the seeds are so tiny, it's recommended you mix them with a bit of sand, sprinkle that on your rich soil and lightly pat. Celery likes to be planted shallowly. Germination can take eight to ten weeks so most gardeners start their plants indoors. *Well* after the last frost (nighttime temperatures don't fall below 50° F), you can move your plants outdoors but watch where you put them. Hot sun or widely varying temperatures will easily kill celery. Again, lots of moisture is necessary.

Notes

CHAMOMILE (GERMAN)
Matricaria recutita

Once upon a time, Roman chamomile (*Chamamelum nobile*) was the favored chamomile. Sometime within the last hundred years or so, that changed and now, although Roman has its *many* uses, German is what you will normally find under the common name, "chamomile." While I stress knowing your Latin binomials to differentiate plants, chamomile can become confusing. The "powers that be" changed their names just a decade or so ago, so you may still find *Anthemis nobilis* describing Roman chamomile and *Matricaria chamomilla* as a synonym for German chamomile.

This is an herb that some non-catnip-loving cats will drool on. Add it to your mixtures to stuff into play mice.

Parts Used Flowers.

Cooking I couldn't find too many instances of chamomile being used in cooking, perhaps due to its peculiar flavor. However, it can be added to beurre blanc, cakes and ice cream.

Medicinal Chamomile has become popular as a sleep aid. Although not a sedative or nervine *per se*, a lot of people swear by a cup of chamomile tea about a half hour before bed. Some migraine sufferers have found relief from a cup or two of tea or a few drops of the tincture. It is a wound healer and combining a few drops of the essential oil with a base oil will quickly calm irritated skin. Wet a cotton swab in a cooled cup of tea and daub the gums of a teething child or to calm the pain of a toothache until you can get to the dentist. **Caution:** May cause allergic reactions to those sensitive to the *Asteraceae* family (the same as ragweed). Excessive doses of chamomile may interfere with anticoagulant therapies; some experts recommend that pregnant and nursing mothers avoid chamomile due to its reputed effects on the menstrual cycle and uterotonic activity.

Magical Due to its calming effect, use chamomile in spells designed to reduce stress. It is a "lucky" herb: use it in money spells; wash hands in chamomile tea before playing cards or gambling; and keep a sachet of chamomile with your lottery tickets. It can be used in spells to combat hexes and curses but the best thing is to deflect those kinds of spells in the first place: hang bunches of it around your house for protection, especially over a baby's crib.

Perhaps due to its apple-like fragrance (the name, chamomile, derives from the Greek for "earth apple"), use chamomile in spells to attract love – add it to your bath water or at the very least, bathe your face in it before going out on a date.

Grow It Yourself German chamomile is an annual so you'll have to replant every year or leave some flowers to go to seed. Even then, you'll want to overseed every couple of years to maintain a full crop. It likes a lot of sun but if you live in a climate where the summers are *hot*, it's probably best to put it in partial shade as it wilts easily. Broadcast the seeds where you want them to grow but do not cover with soil – they need sun to germinate. The soil should be moist but not wet and should drain well. Or be lazy and buy flats of chamomile at the garden center. It usually flowers mid-summer – harvest the tops when the flowers are just opened.

Roman chamomile, on the other hand, is a perennial and will survive all but the harshest winters. It grows much lower (only four to six inches high at maturity) and is often used in place of a lawn.

Notes

CILANTRO/CORIANDER
Coriandrum sativum

Two names, one plant – at least here in North America. Cilantro refers to the leafy part; coriander is the seed. Why *we* have to differentiate on this one plant is beyond me – coriander is the word used for the whole plant in the rest of the world.

Parts Used Aerial, seed.

Cooking Cilantro (the Mexican word for coriander) is used fresh and sparingly – it has a very strong, somewhat citrus-y flavor. It also depends on your tastebuds – to many, it tastes like soap. That said, it reigns supreme as a garnish in Mexican dishes and is used in filled tortillas, in stews and soups, and sprinkled on egg dishes. You can also find the leaves as an ingredient in many Indian, Russian and Chinese dishes (it is also known as Chinese parsley). The seeds are ground (preferably freshly-ground as they lose flavor quickly) and sprinkled on tossed salads, tuna salads and deviled eggs. You may also find it added to butter which is drizzled over steamed vegetables or grilled fish. It may be found as a flavoring agent in some Belgian wheat beers.

Medicinal Chew the seeds right after your meal to cure "garlic breath." An infusion of either the leaves or seeds will help with flatulence, bloating and stomach cramps. Cilantro is high in some antioxidants said to be useful for preventing macular degeneration; one celebrity doctor says that it will help clear heavy metals out of the body.

Magical Coriander is an herb of love. As such, add the seeds to love charms or sachets. Throw coriander seeds at the bride and groom in place of rice. It's said that grinding the seeds and adding them to wine is an effective lust potion. For healing, especially headaches, carry a sachet of the seeds.

The leaves provide protection to gardeners. They also will help promote peace in the home – use them in spells to "clear the air" after an argument or to get two (or more) people to, if not get along, then at least not argue.

Grow It Yourself Plant seeds in a sunny place after the last frost. The type of soil is less important than the fact that it drains well. Like its cousin, celery, it will wilt in *very* hot sun and temperatures consistently above 80° F will cause it to bolt (produce flowers and seeds more quickly than it should), so if necessary, ensure at least partial shade. It likes a moist spring and somewhat dry summer so water sparingly once your plants are established. It is an annual and does not readily re-seed itself so be sure to save some of your coriander seeds to plant the following year instead of eating them all.

Notes

CINNAMON

Cinnamomum verum or *C. cassia*

True cinnamon comes from Sri Lanka and is known as Ceylon cinnamon. What most of us get is cassia cinnamon, which is grown for export in Southeast Asia. There is a slight difference in taste but one only need be concerned about which cinnamon you're consuming if you're on blood-thinning medication. The coumarin content is much, *much* higher in cassia cinnamon. Since we're concerned about finances here, buy the less-expensive cassia cinnamon if you don't have to worry about coumarin.

What we get as "whole" cinnamon (or cinnamon sticks) is actually the inner bark of the tree, which curls as it dries.

Parts Used Inner bark.

Cooking Ah, the baking. I have too many cake and cookie recipes to count that call for cinnamon. Many people mix a little with some sugar and sprinkle that on their buttered morning toast. And who doesn't like a sprinkle of ground cinnamon on their hot chocolate? It's also great on apples, raw or baked. In entrée-type cooking, it adds a little something to stews, curries and chilies. I like it (along with a pinch of nutmeg) with butter on my baked sweet potato or squash. One website even mentioned using it on beef, although I couldn't find a specific recipe.

Medicinal Cinnamon tea is a warming drink for someone who has a cold or the flu. In this case, cinnamon is so strong that you're only going to steep ¼ teaspoon in your cup of hot water. (I usually just smash about ½ inch of a stick with a hammer.) It's one of the recommended herbs for nausea and may calm the stomach enough to stop vomiting. Try some powdered cinnamon in a glass of warm milk to aid digestion, or as a soothing drink for children before bedtime.

Magical A pinch of cinnamon strengthens almost any spell from healing to love to protection to success.

Grow It Yourself If you live in the tropics, you can probably grow yourself a cinnamon tree or two. They will propagate by seed or you may be able to find a root-balled tree in a nursery. It doesn't care what type soil (although it seems to produce a better quality spice in sandy soil) but does want a good amount of moisture. Let your tree grow a couple of years, coppice it, wait another couple of years and once the outer bark is a rich brown, it's ready for harvesting.

Notes

CLOVE

Syzygium aromaticum

Did you know? Those little prickly things that you purchase in the spice aisle at the store are really dried flower buds! One of the tougher and more aromatic herbs, the whole herb will retain its aroma and flavor for *years* if stored properly. Pundits say six months for ground cloves, one year for whole cloves. My supply is five years old and counting, still smells and tastes fresh, and even passes the freshness test (fresh cloves will float vertically in water; old ones either float horizontally or sink).

Parts Used Flower.

Cooking This wonderfully warm herb is most often associated with winter holidays: pumpkin pies, gingerbread, mulled cider, clove-studded baked ham. However, clove is also an ingredient in Jamaican jerk blends, curry powders and the Chinese Five Spices mixture. In France, a clove is inserted into an onion which is then used in making chicken stock. You will find it in many Indian recipes as well as the

Moroccan Ras El Hanout. It is even an ingredient in Worcestershire sauce!

Medicinal Most widely known as an analgesic for a toothache. *One drop* of pure essential oil on a small piece of cotton placed on the offender will kill the pain until you can get to the dentist. Be aware that the taste is *strong* and you may not like it. It's said you can chew a single clove to the same effect but I've never wanted to chew anything hard when a tooth hurts. Your choice.

A few drops in carrier oil can be rubbed onto skin, similar to Vicks VapoRub® to help clear clogged lungs that arise from bronchitis or bronchial asthma. It's a warming herb and that same oil combination will soothe muscle cramps. It's antibacterial so your oil can do triple duty – daub it on acne.

Clove is used in Asia to treat many viral and bacterial illnesses such as malaria and cholera. The oil has also been used for certain fungal infections, such as athlete's foot.

Chew a clove or two to get rid of gas and flatulence.

Magical Add to incenses or burn alone to banish negativity, provide protection and raise the spiritual vibrations of an area. Clove can be used to stop gossip as well as attract riches. Since it is used in spells to comfort the bereaved, I would use it to bring comfort in any situation of loss.

Grow It Yourself Unless you live in a warm, humid, tropical environment, my suggestion is to buy the dried herb from your favorite herb supplier. If you *do* live in such an environment, plant the seeds in partial shade, give them even moisture, then wait about twenty years for the tree to begin flowering.

Notes

CLOVER

Trifolium spp.

Clover comes in all sorts of colors…white, yellow, pink, red… Red (*Trifolium pratense*) is the most medicinally-potent of the genus but you can use any color in a pinch.

Parts Used Flower, leaves.

Cooking As long as no one is spraying chemicals on your lawn, go outside in the spring and pick some clover. You can eat the flowers raw (although some may find them hard to digest), add the young greens to your salad, cook the greens just like any other "cooked green" or fry the flowers as fritters. The whole plant may be added to soups and stews. The dried flowers can be ground and used as a flour (most often sprinkled onto rice).

Medicinal As stated above, red clover is the most medicinally potent so that is what I will address here. It is chock-full of vitamins and minerals and clover tea* is a great boost to those undergoing debilitating chemotherapy or radiation therapy for cancer. That same boost is beneficial to anyone suffering from anemia or any sort of infection. It will help promote milk for nursing mothers. The anti-spasmodic action makes it good for coughs of any kind but especially those associated with bronchitis or a bad cold. **Caution:** Clover has many herb/drug interactions so check with your doctor if you're taking any pharmaceuticals. Drugs that use the same pathway include antiretrovirals and oral contraceptives.

Magical Clover has a strong association with the element of Earth and is especially useful in consecrating tools made of copper (red clover, in this instance). Carry, wear or bathe in it to attract luck, money, love, and success in any undertaking. Place a clover flower in your left shoe to keep evil away from you. Use it in spells to protect and bless domestic animals. It's said if you grow clover in your yard, it will keep snakes away. I think I have immune snakes on my property...

---

* Clover tea should be a *decoction* of the flowers, not an infusion as you would with virtually any other flower.

Grow It Yourself Most people don't have to *plant* clover. A lot of "perfect lawn" folks try to get *rid* of it. However, you can find red clover seeds at a lot of feed stores. It is used by farmers as a cover crop and also as feed for cattle. The seeds should be stratified for several weeks before broadcasting onto your chosen plot just like grass seed. It likes well-drained soil (clay is okay, as long as it drains well), full sun and moderate moisture. While white clover seems to spread rapidly, in my experience, red clover doesn't seem to re-seed itself well, doesn't spread fast and the germination rate even for well-stratified seeds only maxes out at about 75% so you may want to overseed every year or every other year until you have a well-established plot.

You can also gently cut off the stolons (rootlets found just below or just above the surface) from an established plant and, after dipping them in rooting hormone, plant them about three feet away.

Notes

COFFEE

Coffea spp.

Ah, the elixir of life. To me and many others, anyways. Although you may think of it as your morning or afternoon pick-me-up, it has a lot of other uses, too. About 80% of the world's coffee is *Coffea arabica*, although Wikipedia lists 125 different species. One is even *naturally* caffeine-free!

Parts Used Seed.

Cooking Coffee is added to nearly every type of chocolate preparation, up to and including tiramisu. You can find it as a meat marinade or used in braising meats, especially beef and lamb. I've found it as an ingredient in barbeque sauce and in baked beans. Use your imagination! Coffee is slightly bitter so lends itself well to recipes where you may want to take the sweet edge off something.

Medicinal While not generally used in western herbal medicine, coffee can be found in both Ayurvedic and Traditional Chinese Medicine. There, it is used to treat the liver, opening the liver *qi* and alleviating sluggishness. It has an upward/downward effect and when affecting the liver, can affect the spleen and/or gallbladder as well. The Chinese use the green bean to clear out the liver. (Please do consult an Ayurvedic or TCM practitioner before trying this!)

Due to the caffeine content which can be a pain blocker, some migraine sufferers have found relief after drinking a cup or two of strong coffee.

Coffee is a stimulant and apart from the obvious effect of keeping you awake, can promote peristalsis (movement in the colon). The tannins in coffee, however, can be drying and, along with other herbs, are used to treat diarrhea. Although you may find yourself urinating more if you drink a lot of coffee, those tannins are actually dehydrating you, too!

According to many, if you make a paste of coffee grounds and an oil, slather it on your thighs (or wherever) and cover that with plastic wrap for about a half hour, cellulite will disappear after a few treatments. Or just use it as a scrub – rub it on the affected area for about ten minutes before rinsing. In theory, it's the antioxidants that will help get rid of that fat buildup.

Magical The "mental clarity" and stimulation that coffee offers translates itself well to magic. It helps to dispel nightmares and negative thoughts, providing peace of mind. For you professional divinators out there, carry a small jar of coffee grounds with you and take a sniff between readings to clear your mind and replenish your psychic energy. Add brewed coffee to a bath for recuperating from an illness. I've read that burning coffee grounds will repel ghosts. It depends on the ghost, I think. The ones hanging around me *love* coffee in any form!

Grow It Yourself Do you live in the tropics? Preferably at a higher elevation? Then you may be able to grow your own coffee bush. Plant your seeds (two are generally found inside the "cherry") in a shady location, ensure it gets plenty of moisture during the wet season but has a short dry season, as well, then wait. Depending on the species, it will take about four years for the plant to fruit. The rest of us will have to be content with buying our roasted beans (which are really seeds) at the store.

Notes

DANDELION

Taraxacum officinale

Who doesn't know the lowly but ubiquitous dandelion? The bane of every suburban lawn's existence, it's one of my favorite "weeds." Children's, too, if the number of yellow-flower necklaces seen in the spring is any indication.

Parts Used Entire plant.

Cooking The young leaves are added to spring salads. (Ensure they're some of the first to appear...older, larger leaves are quite bitter.) You can sauté those same leaves just as you would any other "green." The blossoms are batter-fried, made into jelly and brewed into wine. The root is roasted, ground and brewed like coffee.

Medicinal Young dandelion leaves or spring-harvested roots are added to spring tonics. Both the leaves and root are a wonderful diuretic. Unlike many other diuretics, they do not deplete potassium levels. As a hepatic, when combined with other herbs, dandelion can be used to treat jaundice. Some herbalists use it in compounds for rheumatoid arthritis. (When harvesting the root be sure to do it in spring or fall, before/after the leaves – that's when all the good compounds gather back down into the root.)

An old wives tale says that a drop or two of the latex (the juice in the stem) will get rid of a wart.

Caution: May cause allergic reactions to those sensitive to the *Asteraceae* family (ragweed). There have been reports of dermatitis in some when the latex in the stem comes in contact with skin.

Magical The first thing that comes to my mind is blowing on the puffball of seeds, asking the seeds to carry your wish on the wind. Others say you can use that same puffball for divination. Count the number of blows it takes to clear the head and that's the number of years you'll live; give the seed head one good blow and however many seeds are left are how long you'll live; or say your ABCs with each blow and your true love's name will start with the letter you said when you clear the head.

The leaves are good for summoning spirits; add to spells for healing, purification or defeating negativity. Add the root to dream pillows for sleep protection; keep it by your bed to enhance your psychic powers. Make an infused oil of the blossoms and massage that oil into your body for manifesting wishes. It's said that adding the leaf or blossom to salads will enhance male fertility.

Grow It Yourself. If you don't have them in your yard and neither does your neighbor (or the neighbor uses chemicals), pick some gone-to-seed flowers from somewhere else, plant and wait. Within a year or two, you'll have more than you could dream of…and so will your neighbors. Dandelion doesn't seem to care about much of anything, except I've noticed they grow better in full sun.

Notes

DILL

Anethum graveolens

When I think of this herb, my mind automatically goes to pickles. But there's so much more…

Parts Used Aerial, seed.

Cooking For the most part, the aerial portion of the plant is used with food. That's what goes into dill pickles. It also makes a wonderful addition to eggs, cheese dishes, vegetables and fish (especially salmon). Dill butter on bread is delicious. The seeds can be used as a caraway substitute.

Medicinal Here, we use the seed. Chew a few seeds for bad breath, or take a cup or two of tea each day for chronic halitosis. (Because chronic halitosis isn't normal, go to your dentist or doctor to find out the root cause.) They're also helpful for digestive disorders such as flatulence. Some have found them helpful in cases of menstrual cramps or painful urination.

Magical So many little seeds make dill useful in luck or money spells. Because employment generally equals money, use it in workings for getting a job. The scent is said to stimulate lust so add a cup or two of tea to your bath water before a date. Men: to attract women, hang a muslin bag filled with seed from your showerhead and allow the water to flow through it and onto you. It's effective at repelling negativity: place a sprig at your door, or carry a piece or a few seeds on you in a muslin bag.

Grow It Yourself Dill is a beautiful, tall, feathery perennial that is good for your garden, attracting bees and other beneficial insects. It's easy to grow in most any climate. It likes warm, rich earth so plant it directly into your garden (or outdoor pot) in early summer when the soil stays warm even at night, covering with about one-quarter inch of dirt. Thin about two weeks after leaves appear. It will readily self-seed. Dill is a good companion plant for cabbage or onions but it and carrots don't get along.

Notes

ELDER

Sambucus nigra, S. canadensis

Not for the first time is there disagreement among botanists. Some say that there are two species of black elder; some say there's only one. (There are many others elder species; we'll only concern ourselves with the two most-used in a medicinal sense.)

Parts Used Fruit, flowers.

Cooking All green parts of the plant are mildly poisonous – including the unripe berries! When ripe, the berries are *quite* tart and need to be cooked. Otherwise, you can use them as you would most any other berry in jellies, chutneys, pies or condiments. They also make an interesting glaze for pork or beef dishes. There is even a traditional Scandinavian soup made from elderberries.

The flowers are used to make cordials or a syrup which is diluted before drinking. There are several commercial elderflower beverages on the market. You can also fry the flowers to make fritters.

And of course, there are various alcoholic beverages made with either the berries or flowers, including a type of champagne.

Medicinal The berries make an excellent syrup used to treat colds, coughs and the flu. If you can't make your own, there is a commercial product called Sambucol® that works quite well. A tincture or infusion of the flowers is diaphoretic and may also help with the above issues. Make an ointment of the leaves (heating long enough to crisp the leaves) for sprains and chilblains.

Magical Elder is one of the best magical herbs I've encountered. The shrub (or small tree) is considered a "threshold tree" – it is either a doorway to the Otherworld or stands at that door – depending on who you ask, of course. It is said fairies inhabit elder so be doubly respectful when harvesting any part of it.

The wood is used during death rites and in protection rituals. Many protective amulets are carved from its wood.

The flowers may be added to dream pillows to enhance sleep and provide protection.

Drinking a beverage made from elder from a shared glass will "seal the deal" during an engagement. After marriage, place a branch beneath your bed to preserve that love, stimulate passion and protect against the temptation of adultery.

Be warned: elder is a picky herb and may act contrary to your wishes if it doesn't favor you.

Grow It Yourself Elder isn't too concerned about its soil but will do better in something loamy rather than sandy. It will tolerate cold and wet (it grows in Canada!) and will easily die during a drought. It is usually propagated by hardwood or softwood cuttings that put out new rootlets within a couple of weeks. While I've read that it will survive in full sun, I've noticed here in the southern woods it grows in partial shade. Even a mature shrub has shallow roots so needs to be well-mulched or attended to keep weeds from competing for soil nutrients.

If properly cared for, your elder tree will put out berries the first year but they'll be rather puny. These you should leave for the birds and wait until the second year to harvest for a meatier crop.

Notes

EUCALYPTUS

Eucalyptus spp.

No one is more loving of eucalyptus leaves than a koala. Those leaves are the *only* thing they eat and being approximately 55% water, eucalyptus provides most of their water requirements, too. The koalas are lucky: the leaf contains a cyanide compound and they are one of few mammals whose body has adapted to digesting that poison.

It's said that the scent of eucalyptus repels cockroaches.

Parts Used Leaves.

Cooking I'd never thought about adding what I consider to be a cold medicine to food but according to one Australian website, the leaf is a final addition when smoking meats – especially fish. Australians also put a small amount in potato dishes, add a leaf when making jelly or a drop of the essential oil in a meringue to top berries.

Medicinal Its pungent smell is stimulating (to say the least), and it is an ingredient in many cold and flu preparations to help bring down fevers and expel mucus. A few drops of the essential oil in a vaporizer may help open the airways of those suffering from asthma or bronchitis. (I just open the bottle and inhale.) There are several different species of eucalyptus used in a medicinal sense...my professors recommended that *Eucalyptus radiata* essential oil be used instead of *E. globulus* when treating children. It's milder and has a slightly minty undertone.

Magical Use eucalyptus in all sorts of healing spells but especially those concerned with colds. It also confers protection and will purify any space.

Grow It Yourself There are over 700 eucalyptus species; all but nine are found in Australia. A native of temperate-to-tropical regions, the vast majority do not tolerate frost and only a few will survive temperatures below 23° F (5° C). It will grow in almost any soil, although it likes a somewhat saline environment. As a water-lover, eucalyptus has been planted to reduce the water table in some areas. It is also considered invasive in some parts of the world as it grows quickly and will take over an area, similar to bamboo.

Notes

FENNEL

Foeniculum vulgare

A member of the *Apiaceae* (dill) family, fennel can bring beauty to a garden with its tall, feathery leaves. The whole plant has a licorice-y aroma and attracts bees and other beneficial insects. While we may think of only seeds, the whole plant can be used.

Parts Used Aerial, seed.

Cooking Fennel grows very much like its relative, celery, and the bottom of the stalks form a bulb that can be shredded and added to salads or side dishes. It can be braised with chicken or fish, or pureed and added to soups or sauces. Chop the stalks and add them to salads as you would celery or cook them in stir-fry or pastas. The seed is used to flavor fish, breads and chutneys.

Medicinal Chew the seeds as a breath freshener. For flatulence, drink a cup of tea made from the seeds about a half hour before eating. The same tea will aid a sluggish digestion. Although the medical community isn't sure what causes it, colic is generally the result of something wrong with a baby's digestive system. A quarter-cup of tea may help ease baby's distress (and Mom's, too).

Magical The seeds, as usual for seeds, are used in fertility spells, especially those concerned with male virility. They are used in purification and healing rituals. Hang a bag of seeds or a stalk in windows and doors to ward off evil or grow some around your house to confer whole-house protection. Scott Cunningham said putting a piece of fennel in your left shoe will prevent ticks from biting your legs.

Grow It Yourself While it's actually a perennial, fennel is grown as an annual to harvest the entire plant. You can plant seeds after the last frost in full sun but be aware that they will be slow to germinate. It can also be propagated by dividing the roots or the bulb at the base of the plant. It will grow in almost any soil with moderate water requirements.

Fennel doesn't play well with others so do not plant it with any herb other than dill.

Notes

FENUGREEK

Trigonella foenum-graecum

This sweet plant's Latin name translates to "Greek Hay", probably because it was grown for cattle feed, along with clover and vetch, in Cato the Elder's day. It's been around longer than that: charred seeds found in Iran have been carbon dated to 4000 BCE.

Parts Used Seed.

Cooking A little goes a long way! You can dry-roast the seeds or fry them in oil before adding to your dish. The leaves and seeds are generally used sparingly in vegetable dishes, especially spinach and potatoes. It is an ingredient in curries, pickles, chutneys and many other preparations from the Near and Middle East. The young leaves are sold as "methi" and used similar to sprouts or microgreens.

Medicinal This is another seed you can chew to get rid of bad breath. (They're *hard*. Grind or crush them a little, first, to prevent breaking a tooth.) The seeds are taken internally to encourage weight gain, soothe gastritis, induce childbirth and encourage milk production in nursing mothers. A paste of the ground seeds can be applied to abscesses, boils or other skin eruptions. The tea can be used as a douche in the treatment of leucorrhea.

Medicinal *Money, money, money!* Used in various spells to attract money into your life, the most popular being: half-fill a jar with seeds and leave it open on your desk (or wherever you pay your bills). Add a few seeds every day until the jar is full. Empty the jar outside and start over. Add a few seeds to the water you use to wash your floors to attract money to the household.

As with all small seeds, they can be used in fertility spells, too.

Grow It Yourself Fenugreek is an annual and will grow in most climates. It is slow to start and will probably do best if you start it indoors several weeks before the last frost. As a legume, it doesn't like to be transplanted so use biodegradable pots (cardboard egg cartons do well) that can be put directly into the soil after the last frost. It prefers full sun to partial shade, a loamy, well-drained soil and moderate water.

Notes

FLAX

Linum usitatissimum

You knew flax is the source of the fabric linen, right? The fibers of the plant have been woven into cloth for at least 30,000 years. The oil (pressed from the seed) is used in woodworking and is known as linseed (or flaxseed) oil. The Latin species name *usitatissimum* means "most useful."

Parts Used Seed, oil.

Cooking Flax seeds are high in fiber and omega-3 fatty acids. They have a slightly nutty flavor and whole seeds can be added to your breakfast cereal or to homemade muffins, cookies and breads. They are a side dish all their own in northern India. Grind them and sprinkle on cooked vegetables or add them to your morning smoothie. (The whole seeds will keep well but ground flax will go rancid quickly unless packed immediately in an airtight container. Grind and use fresh.)

You can add a tablespoon of *food grade* linseed/flaxseed oil to your smoothie, soups or vegetarian entrees. The oil used in woodworking has probably been extracted by solvent. You don't want to ingest that.

Medicinal Flax seeds have been used in Ayurvedic medicine for thousands of years. Due to the high fiber content, they are useful for constipation and sluggish digestion. Austrians have used the seeds either internally or externally to treat respiratory issues, infections, and gout. In the highlands of Scotland, a poultice of flaxseeds is applied as a general cure for any kind of swelling. **Caution:** Flaxseeds can affect the absorption of other drugs. Also, despite their use as a laxative, consuming large quantities of the seeds without drinking plenty of water can *cause* constipation.

Magical Like most seeds, they are used in money spells. Perhaps due to the oil content, they (or the oil) can be used in beauty spells. Sprinkle some around the house for protection or around your table before reading cards to get a more accurate reading. (Or you can drink a cup of tea before divining.) Add them to healing rituals, too.

Egyptian priests wore only linen because flax was considered a symbol of purity. Their mummies are wrapped in it, too. Perhaps because of that purity symbolism or maybe because linen was *the* fabric of choice in the Middle East until cotton was commercialized in the early 20th century. Use a linen cloth on your altar when "purity" is a consideration.

Grow It Yourself Flax will grow just about anywhere. It is grown just like a cereal crop – with the plants close together. It likes cool weather best so sow anywhere from January to May, depending on your climate, in full sun. Cover with ½" or so of soil. You'll get a better crop if your soil is fertile and well-drained. Germination takes about ten days and it'll be about four months to harvest. It is an annual so after those gorgeous flowers disappear and you get seeds, be sure to save some for the following year.

Notes

GARLIC AND ONION

Allium sativum and. A. cepa

Who doesn't know these two vegetables/herbs/spices? (Take your pick...they're all of them.) They are staples in most everyone's kitchen. Fresh is best unless you want powder, in which case, cut them up into small pieces and dry them thoroughly before running them through your grinder.

Parts Used Bulb.

Cooking Both herbs are grown all over the world and used in virtually every type of cuisine.

Medicinal The list of therapeutic properties for garlic is almost as long as my arm. It really shines in anything having to do with boosting the immune system...I recommend everyone eat a couple of cloves a day as a preventive measure. Some people can't stomach raw garlic but can handle raw onions. Onions are good in this regard, too. If your stomach doesn't like either, try garlic pearls found in the supplement section at the store. They've had the stomach-irritating compound removed. This takes out some of the beneficial qualities, but not all.

Garlic-infused oil has been used for centuries to help earaches. Warm onion juice will help an earache, too. Just put a few drops of either into the affected ear, let it sit for a few minutes and then tilt your head to allow the liquid to run out. The same infused oil or juice can be taken on a daily basis to help with fatigue and increase stamina.

Foods with raw garlic and/or onion in them are great for colds: they'll help bring down any fevers and start breaking up the mucus that causes congestion, both in your lungs and in your nose. A poultice of either will accomplish the same thing but beware: the raw vegetable and even the juice can cause blistering and contact dermatitis. Apply a cut clove of garlic or slice of onion to spot-treat acne.

It is said if you put slices of raw onion on the bottom of your feet overnight (wear socks to bed to keep them there), you'll break up a cold almost immediately. The soles of your feet have a lot of pores and absorb chemicals easily.

Magical Use either garlic or onion in any healing or protection spell. Be sure to store them in the kitchen to keep illness from starting there. Put a cut onion in the four corners of a sickroom to absorb negativity and disease. Dispose of them in running water when they turn black.

To induce lust, use plenty of fresh garlic or onion in your cooking.

Cunningham said placing an onion under your pillow will induce prophetic dreams. I'm not sure I'd dream at all: the lump of the onion coupled with the aroma would probably keep me awake! You can certainly try it, though.

Grow It Yourself Both will grow just about anywhere, as long as the soil isn't wet. There are specialty sites on the Internet where you can buy gourmet garlic but a bulb you buy at the grocery store will work just fine. Separate the cloves and plant them shallowly, point-up. Garlic is a great companion plant for roses – it deters aphids.

Onions will grow from seeds but the seeds need to be fresh and these are difficult to find. What you will find are "sets" or starter bulbs. These also should be planted shallowly – cover with an inch or less of dirt.

For both: Because the roots don't spread, you can place them amongst other plants. They only need four to six inches of space. They will be more pungent if the soil is loamy and gardeners suggest adding a nitrogen fixative to the soil before planting. Moisture is necessary but if the soil is constantly wet, your bulbs will rot, so ensure it drains well.

Once the leaves start to droop or turn brown, push or stomp them all the way to the ground to hasten the ripening process of the bulb. Once you harvest them, let them dry on a screen for a week or two before putting into storage. Your storage area should be cool and dry to prevent sprouting.

Notes

GINGER

Zingiber officinale

I don't know for certain but my thought is that the Latin name for this herb is where we get the English word "zing" from. It's definitely zingy! This is an herb that has a lot of cautions associated with it. If you have health issues, please do some research before taking it internally. (A pinch in cooking should be fine.)

Parts Used Root.

Cooking Ginger ale, ginger beer, ginger brandy...oh wait, we're talking about food. Okay, ginger snaps, gingerbread, ginger candy... You'll find ginger as an ingredient in sweet and savory dishes, marinades and stir-fries. It's a staple in Asian cuisine. I also found mention of ginger macaroni and cheese, ginger plus just about any vegetable or fruit, and ginger custard or ice cream.

Medicinal Ginger is famous as an anti-nausea herb and is suggested for both morning and motion sickness. A piece of ginger candy can help, as can drinking a cup of lukewarm (not hot) ginger tea.

It can be used in cases of stopped menses or painful menses but please check with your doctor first – there's always a reason these things happen and using ginger could exacerbate another issue. Because it's useful for these conditions, you and your doctor should weigh the risks of using ginger for anything if you're pregnant – even morning sickness.

Ginger is a warming herb and I find it useful for the chills that accompany the flu. As well, the pungency is great for breaking up congestion. Once upon a time, in the days before "stay home if you're sick so you don't spread germs," I was a waitress in a bar. I had contracted a horrible cold: my nose was stopped up and I had a scratchy throat. The owner of the bar warmed a shot of ginger brandy, had me inhale the fumes and then drink the brandy. Within minutes, I could breathe and my throat felt better. (The shot of alcohol certainly made the rest of my shift more pleasant!)

Caution: As mentioned above, this herb has a lot of contraindications. It has several potential drug interactions so be sure to check with your physician before using it to treat a health issue or overindulging on ginger food.

Magical Ginger adds a little 'oomph' to any spell and if you eat a piece of root before performing that spell, it'll give you a boost, too. Powdered ginger is sprinkled around an office or other place of business to draw success (which, in theory, means money).

Use ginger to attract some *zing* into your life: adventure, joy and fun. Carry a small piece of root on you or infuse an oil which you can then use as a personal anointment or to dress candles or other magical items used in a spell for such.

Grow It Yourself You can grow ginger in a *large* pot in the house, or outdoors if you live in a temperate climate. You can buy starter roots or just get a good-sized root from the grocery store. Soak your root overnight, then cut it into smaller chunks. (Roots will generally have nodes on them – these are "buds" – don't cut those.) Plant shallowly in well-drained soil in partial shade and ensure the temperature stays around 75-85° F. Water lightly, then a little more heavily when shoots appear, cutting back to almost no water in the winter when the plant is dormant. Ginger matures in about a year – your indication that you can harvest is when the aerial part of the plant is about two feet tall. It will also send up small sprouts around the main plant – dig these up and replant them for even more ginger.

Notes

HAWTHORN

Crataegus spp.

Not normally an herb you'd associate with a kitchen cupboard, you say? Read on…

Parts Used Flowering tops, fruit (berries), leaves.

Cooking While sometimes quite tart or so sweet they're compared to an over-ripe apple (depending on the species), the haws (berries) are used in jellies and jams, and in making wine and other alcoholic beverages. A soup is also made with the berries. In Mexico, a paste made from the berries is mixed with sugar and chili powder to make a popular candy. (Remove the seeds from the berries before using.) Very young spring leaves can be added to salads. Those leaves, along with the flower buds, are eaten as a trailside snack when hiking, and are called "Bread and Cheese" in rural England.

Medicinal Hawthorn has been used in Traditional Chinese Medicine as a digestive aid. European species have been used for years to strengthen cardiovascular function and are now used in western herbal medicine to help restore blood pressure to normal levels; to treat atherosclerosis; and to lower cholesterol levels. Some have found it a helpful sedative. **Caution:** Hawthorn can produce major drug interactions. Check with your physician before using. Do not use with any other cardiovascular herbs due to the unpredictability of effects and adverse effects.

Magical Hawthorn is used in fertility magic – the flowering branches are including in weddings and handfastings to increase fertility. Conversely, it can be used to enhance chastity and contraception.

An old Roman custom was to have *flaming* hawthorn branches in the nuptial bedroom to ensure the marriage was a happy one. Not sure I'd try this one at home! Perhaps just hang the branches on the headboard or place them around the room.

Staying on the happiness theme, sprinkle an infusion of the flowers around the house to repel and remove negative vibrations or entities.

Grow It Yourself Check with your local garden center to determine which species will grow well in your climate. You also want to think about size – some species are small shrubs while others may be a small tree, gaining fifteen or more feet in height. As a generality, hawthorn likes well-drained, slightly acidic soil and full sun. Most hawthorns are propagated by hardwood cuttings but seeds can be planted as well. If you plant seeds, do so in the fall and expose the seed to the rigors of winter. Propagation by seed is an iffy proposition and it may be a year or more before your seeds germinate.

Notes

HOPS

Humulus lupulus

This is one herb that is best stored in a vacuum-sealed bag in your freezer rather than in a cupboard. Hops age rapidly and the best beer brewers say they'll go bad in about six months if not frozen (preferably in a freezer that doesn't get opened often so they're not exposed to much light).

Parts Used Flowers.

Cooking Apart from beer, hops can be used in recipes that call for bay leaves, oregano and tarragon. They've found their way into cornbread fritters, braised short ribs and even ice cream! Whole hop flowers can be breaded and fried as a tempura, or blended into a cream sauce used to top chicken or pasta. Combine some lemon juice and powdered hops to sprinkle on baking fish for a different flavor.

Medicinal Most people know that hops are a soporific: they'll put you to sleep. However, use them where a calming effect is needed: nervous tension, tension headache, anxiety or an upset stomach. My professors said that fresh hops are best for medicinal applications. **Caution:** Do not use with marked depression as the sedative effects may accentuate symptoms. They may also increase the effects of alcohol or sedative medications.

Magical Most often associated with spells to promote sleep and in dream pillows. They can also be used in healing work and to bring serenity to a person or area.

Grow It Yourself Not recommended for indoor pots! Hops need *a lot* of space, as the vines can grow as much as a foot a day. They require full sun, a loamy, neutral or slightly alkaline soil and plenty of nutrients (manure applications are recommended). Ensure there's a tall trellis or something for the vines to grow on. I can't find an instance of seeds for sale – rhizomes (rootlets) are available. These can be started indoors and transplanted once the danger of frost has passed. Hops are perennial so once you get them started, you should have a lifetime supply – some plants will produce two or more pounds of flowers per year.

Notes

HOREHOUND

Marrubium vulgare

Horehound is an acquired taste and I'm one of those who have acquired it. Horehound cough drops were *the* thing when I was a kid and I could eat them like candy. I don't see them on the shelf at the local store anymore but they're still one of my "go-to" solutions for coughs-due-to-colds so I make my own.

Parts Used Flowering tops, leaves.

Cooking I'd only heard of horehound as an ingredient in the cocktail, Rock and Rye (there's also horehound beer) so I was surprised to find it mentioned in so many types of dishes. It's used as a rub for seafood, fish and game preparations; as a green in salads; with other aromatic herbs in sauces like pesto; as a compliment to dishes with crumbly cheeses such as feta; and on and on. My suggestion would be if you would normally use an aromatic herb (perhaps mint or thyme) in a dish, try horehound. At least once.

Medicinal As mentioned above, it's one of my "go-to" herbs for coughs of almost any kind and/or the lung congestion that accompanies the common cold or bronchitis. It's a bitter so may be used to stimulate appetite. **Caution:** Contact with the fresh plant juice may cause dermatitis. Excessive doses will cause nausea and/or diarrhea and have been known to cause heart arrhythmia.

Magical Horehound is an extremely protective herb: carry or hang to ward off sorcery and fascination, or scatter during a home blessing. Add it to a healing sachet. An infusion will help with focus during rituals, stimulate personal creativity and balance personal energies. Or add that infusion to your bath to enhance a healing spell.

Grow It Yourself Horehound is a perennial. It *can* be grown from seed but germination is difficult. Better is either cuttings or root division. It's a member of the mint family so can easily take over a bed but makes a wonderful companion plant for tomatoes and peppers and will attract beneficial insects. It likes full sun, well-drained soil and even moisture. Soil *quality* isn't as important as drainage. Once established, don't overwater.

Notes

HYSSOP

Hyssopus officinalis

Hyssop is grown *just* for its gorgeous blue flowers but this plant is so much more than pretty. It's mentioned several times in the Christian Bible so its purification and protective properties have been known for a couple of millennia.

Parts Used Flowering herb.

Cooking The flowers and leaves are edible and used like other fresh herbs in salads, pastas and soups. Use with a little lemon juice as a finishing touch for stocks. Replace all or some of the mint with hyssop in lamb recipes. It's combined with some cheeses; baked into bread; added to glazes (especially for vegetables such as carrots); infused into custards, puddings or ice cream; made into jams and candies… Wherever you might use a delicate herb, try hyssop.

Medicinal Hyssop really shines in getting rid of infections, whether it be viral like the common cold or bacterial, such as a wound (if used as a poultice, it'll also help heal that wound).

It's useful for bringing down fevers, breaking up congestion and getting rid of a phlegmy cough.

An oil infused with hyssop is a good massage oil, especially for healing touch therapies.

Magical It's one of the most widely-used purification herbs. Add the dried herb or flowers to sachets; scatter around a home or sprinkle the infusion around to clear negativity from an area. Use that same infusion to cleanse ritual items, your sacred space and yourself. It's said to deter thieves so grow it around your house or store it with your precious items.

The branches are quite stiff so you can use them to sprinkle other infusions around. (In the Roman Catholic and Anglican churches, this is known as an aspergillum. You don't need any fancy tools.)

Grow It Yourself Start seeds inside about eight weeks before the last frost or buy seedlings at your local garden center. It prefers full sun but isn't picky about its soil as long as it's well-drained, making it a perfect addition to rock gardens. It is a perennial that can grow two feet or more high and as a member of the mint family, it will take over an area so be careful where you plant it.

The plant is very woody so makes a wonderful hedge-y border. However, it does get a little *too* woody after a few years and some gardeners suggest replacing your plants every four years or so.

Notes

IRISH MOSS
Chondrus crispus

I'd never heard of this herb until I started herbalist school. It's *marvelous*. It's not a moss; it's actually a red algae whose color ranges from yellow to deep purple. You might also find it as carrageen moss. (Be careful…there is a perennial green herb that goes by this common name but is a member of the *Sagina* genus.)

Parts Used The whole plant.

Cooking It is an ingredient in a Jamaican drink called "Put the Lead Back," which is said to enhance libido. Apart from that, it can be used as a thickener for just about anything such as puddings or ice cream. It can also be used in salads and in bread. It and another seaweed are used to produce the chemical carrageenan, which is a commercial thickener.

It is used as a clarifying agent in brewing beer and wine. When mixed with the wort, it will attract solids to it, making the brew easier to strain.

Medicinal A decoction of the dried plant (flavor it with something like lemon, ginger or cinnamon) is very useful as an expectorant. It has a mucilaginous quality so your decoction will turn to jelly as it cools – drink it hot! That same mucilage is soothing, making it a useful addition to preparations for urinary tract infections.

In Venezuela, it is boiled with milk, sweetened with honey and given before bedtime to soothe sore throats and ease chest congestion.

Magical An excellent herb for luck (and money), carry it with you or put a couple of pieces under your rugs to ensure a steady flow of luck (and money) into your home or business. Add it to any luck oil to enhance its properties. It's an excellent herb for gamblers – either carry it in a pouch or drink a decoction before sitting down to a table of cards or dice.

Grow It Yourself If you live near or visit the Atlantic Ocean in the northern hemisphere, you should have no difficulty finding some of this and shouldn't have to grow it yourself. It can be found growing on rocks from the middle intertidal area all the way to the ocean floor. If you're a landlubber, buy it dried from a reputable source.

Notes

JASMINE

Jasminum officinale

Ah, one of the sweetest smells. Did you know? The flowers are so tiny and the amount of volatile oil so little that it takes approximately 227,000 hand-picked blossoms to make one ounce of essential oil. There is so little volatile oil that dried flowers carry effectively no scent.

The genus name is derived from the Persian Yasameen ("gift from God").

Parts Used Flowers.

Cooking Despite its name, jasmine rice isn't infused with the flower. It's actually a type of long-grain rice. (Although I suppose you could cook your plain ol' white rice in an infusion of the flowers...) You can find jasmine in ice cream, in syrups, in drinks (usually as an addition to another beverage, such as Tea), in a vinaigrette over a spring salad, or one recipe I found soaks lemon cake layers in a jasmine infusion, which sounds very tasty.

Medicinal Widely known as a nervine – a calmative, if you will. One cup of an infusion a day will help with anxiety, irritability or nervous tension.

Magical Although known as an herb of love, it's usually used for a spiritual rather than a physical attraction. Carry in a sachet or burn as an incense to attract wealth or promote new ideas; the same sachet under your pillow or incense burned before bed will help bring on prophetic dreams. Add a few drops of the essential oil to a massage oil or a cup of infusion to your bath to repair a damaged aura.

Grow It Yourself There are over two hundred jasmine species: some are evergreen, some are deciduous, some are trees or shrubs, and some are vines. Find out from your local horticultural office which species will grow well in your climate and follow the growing instructions carefully. As a generality, they all like full sun to partial shade, a mild climate and a fertile, well-drained soil.

Notes

JUNIPER

Juniperus communis

As I like to grow not just pretty but useful plants, I got excited when I saw some juniper shrubs at the garden center until I got the sales associate to look up the Latin binomial (it wasn't on the tag – shame on them). It was a cultivar of *Juniperus sabina*, which is poisonous. Juniper is one plant you really need to know what you're getting. They're not all interchangeable.

Parts Used Bark, berries (which are actually the seed cones), leaves.

Cooking The leaves and berries are used extensively in cooking. The leaves (needles) have a slightly rosemary-ish taste with a hint of citrus and can be used with lamb, pork and wild meats such as rabbit or venison. The berries can be used fresh or dried, whole or crushed and may be found as flavorings in casseroles, marinades and stuffings, and even in sauerkraut. You'll also find them in sweet dishes, like fruitcake. Oh, and they're the original ingredient in gin – the

Dutch word for juniper is jenever and it was originally a medicinal drink.

Medicinal Juniper is widely known as a helper in the urinary system and is included in preparations for bladder inflammation, leucorrhea and candida infections. Used both internally and externally, some who suffer from sciatica or arthritis have found relief. It is also a bitter tonic and may help in cases of indigestion. **Caution:** It is a reported abortifacient and affects the menstrual cycle. It is a diuretic and prolonged use may lead to low potassium levels. Do not use for more than four to six weeks without taking a two week break. May increase the efficacy of hypoglycemic and diuretic therapies.

Magical Either wearing a string of the berries or adding a juniper infusion to your bath water will attract love. (Ladies, you can also use diluted infused vinegar as a douche for the same purpose.) A shrub growing by the front door or a sprig hung over that door will protect the home from theft. Overall, juniper banishes bad things and attracts good things: health, energy, love, protection. The leaves smell wonderful in incense.

Grow It Yourself Various species and cultivars of juniper can be found throughout the northern hemisphere. Some are upright shrubs to small trees; some are "creeping" and make excellent ground cover. As a general rule, juniper likes full sun and *well-drained* soil. If you buy seeds, they need to be cold-stratified for three to four months before planting.

Notes

LAVENDER

Lavandula angustifolia or *L. officinalis*

Two plants, interchangeable. While medicinal in its own right and probably interchangeable in magical applications, the one you don't want in cookery is *L. x intermedia*, which is Lavandin. The flowers are a brighter blue-purple than true lavender but they have a slight camphor overtone to them.

Parts Used Flowers.

Cooking Fresh or dried, lavender flowers add a subtle note to sweets. Add a handful of flower spikes to a few cups of granulated sugar in a sealed container, allow a week or so for them to infuse, then use that sugar to flavor teas or baked goods. Recipes for lavender custard, lavender syrup (yummy on berries) and baked goods of all kinds abound. If you grow it yourself, use the stems for kebabs – they're not sweet like the flowers but slightly bitter and will add an interesting note to your meat.

Medicinal Just the aroma of lavender is said to cure bouts of (non-clinical) depression. For everyday stress or a tension headache, a cup of lavender tea is just the thing. (Be aware: the tea isn't a pretty blue-purple. It's light green!) For that same headache, rubbing a couple of drops of lavender essential oil on your temples provides relief. Lavender essential oil is one of two or three that you can use on your skin without dilution (but don't ever take it internally unless you're under the guidance of a certified aromatherapist).

Magical Use lavender when you want to bring peace and harmony to a situation – either a whole house or between two participants in an argument. It's great in dream pillows to promote restful sleep. Cunningham said the scent of lavender attracts men, so use it in love sachets. You can also infuse lavender in a bottle of white wine and serve it as a love potion.

Grow it Yourself Lavender is a perennial that will grow in zones 5 and above but if you have harsh winters, you may want to consider either planting it in pots that you bring indoors during the worst months or covering your garden plants.

While seeds are available, your best bet is to buy seedlings from your local nursery. It likes full sun, a moderate amount of moisture and *well-drained*, slightly alkaline soil. Lavender will die quickly from root rot if its feet are wet. As a matter of fact, wet, humid summers kill more lavender plants than cold winters. In a garden, ensure plenty of spacing between plants (a foot or more) to allow good air circulation.

Notes

LEMON

Citrus limon

When life hands you lemons, grab the tequila bottle. Oh wait, I think I meant "make lemonade." Or you could add the juice of one of them to a spray bottle of water to clean and disinfect your kitchen counters. The juice is said to bleach freckles, too.

If you want to write secret notes, use lemon juice as your ink. It will disappear on drying but can be made visible again by heating the paper (traditionally, holding it high over a candle flame).

Parts Used The entire fruit, juice and peel.

Cooking Lemon is used in everything from baking to meat and vegetable dishes. It's said to be a "flavor catalyst", meaning it interacts with your taste buds to enhance the flavors that follow. A squeeze of fresh lemon juice can be used on just about anything. And don't forget the rind! Grate a little into risottos, pastas, stews and puddings. (But grate only the yellow part of the rind. The white pith doesn't taste very good.)

Medicinal Equal parts of hot water and lemon juice with a spoonful of honey makes an excellent remedy for a sore throat or a dry cough. This preparation is said to be used by professional singers to open their throat prior to a performance. The same could be said for those who talk for a living – teachers and lecturers. For a cold with a cough that keeps you awake, my grandfather recommended adding a shot of whiskey to that water/lemon combination before bed.

If you don't like the smell of lavender, try inhaling the aroma of some lemon juice or lemon essential oil to help a tension headache.

Diluted lemon juice will ease the pain of a sunburn. It's a refrigerant but the acid in the juice will help restore the skin to its natural pH balance. (If your lemonade doesn't have any sugar in it, you can dump your glass on yourself. If it does, don't. Sugar will make the burn hurt worse.) Lemon juice also makes an excellent facial astringent. The juice is sticky, so rinse your face with cold water afterwards. That will rinse the juice off and help to close pores.

Magical Use a combination of juice and water (or essential oil and water) to cleanse your tools, amulets, jewelry ... anything you've purchased secondhand. If you have peel leftover from something else, you can soak that in water for a few hours and use it as a wash, too. Add the juice to a purification bath, especially those taken at the full moon.

If you have a tree handy, a few leaves can be steeped in water and drunk as a tea to provoke lust. Dried flowers or peel can be added to love sachets and mixtures.

Lemons get bitter as they age so use the juice of an almost-rotten fruit to cause bitterness. Or write the name of the person you don't like on a piece of paper, pin that to a fresh lemon and wait. As the fruit rots, the person will get less and less happy.

Grow It Yourself Citrus fruits are warmth lovers. If you live in a climate where freezing rarely occurs, you can have a tree outdoors. Otherwise, you'll need a *large* pot that you can bring indoors in the winter months. Trees can grow as high as 22 feet but there are dwarf varieties available that will only reach 8 to 12 feet.

As long as your fruit hasn't been refrigerated, you can start a tree from seed. Soak your seeds overnight in water, then plant them about ½" deep in a pot of rich potting soil. Cover with plastic to keep it moist and warm and put the pot in a sunny window until you see a sprout. Remove the plastic and plant outdoors in a sunny location that is sheltered from wind. Grafted trees generally begin bearing fruit around 3 to 5 years old; trees grown from seed may take ten years or more.

Notes

LEMON BALM

Melissa officinalis

This is one of a myriad of plants that goes by the common name "balm". Be sure you add the "lemon" in front or do as I do and refer to it as "melissa." Melissa is the Greek word for "bee" and it produces small, fragrant flowers that do indeed attract bees.

Parts Used Aerial.

Cooking While the above-ground portion of the plant is used medicinally and magically, only the leaves are used in cooking – and fresh ones, at that. (The dried leaves retain very little of their lemony scent and flavor.) Use them in place of lemon peel in sauces, soups, vinaigrettes and in seafood dishes. They can be added to a green salad or tossed with mixed fruit. Make herb butter with the leaves and then use that in dishes that have butter as an ingredient. Bake cookies, bread or scones with finely-chopped leaves. Infuse the fresh plant in water (as a sun tea) for a refreshing pick-me-up after a hard day in the garden or yard.

Medicinal Melissa is one of the best natural remedies for herpes simplex (cold sores). Make a lotion or lip balm with a melissa-infused oil to daub on those painful spots. That same lotion will also ease the pain of shingles, which are from the chickenpox virus (herpes zoster). An infusion of the leaves will help with flatulence and dyspepsia. Melissa is an ingredient in Carmelite Water, an old, very tasty tonic that was used for headaches and "nervous complaints." **Caution:** May interfere with the action of thyroid hormone therapy.

Magical Very useful in healing spells, especially those suffering from mental or nervous disorders. The Arabians used it in love spells and yet others in workings for success. Steep some leaves in a bottle of white wine for a few days, strain and use that either as a potion or drink it during your ritual.

Grow It Yourself As a member of the mint family, melissa will grow just about anywhere and take over not only its allotted spot but its neighbors', too. It seems to like partial sun better than full – I've found it gets sunburned easier than its cousins. Harvest before or after, but not during flowering for the strongest flavor.

Notes

LEMONGRASS
Cymbopogon citratus

To be honest, I'd never heard of lemongrass until a friend sent me a selection of spices she had picked up on her Asian travels. Once I opened the package, I fell in love. As it's named, it has a lovely lemony scent, similar to but much stronger than melissa.

Parts Used Leaves.

Cooking When buying it dried, you generally get only the leaves. In the produce section of your grocery store, however, you'll find the entire aerial portion of the plant. It's a tough plant and you'll want to cut it into one- or two-inch pieces then crush it with the side of a knife prior to using it to release the volatile oils.

It also holds up well to cooking: if you want a strong flavor in your dish, add it at the start. If you want a lighter, fresher flavor, add it near the end of cooking. If you use the stalks in cooking, remove them before serving – they're rather woody.

Lemongrass lends itself well to marinades, stir-fries, meat rubs, salads and curry pastes.

Medicinal It's a pain reliever, a sedative and a fever reducer. South American folk medicine used the grass for treating hypertension, inflammation, nervousness, sleep disorders, infection, fevers and gastrointestinal disorders. However, it can cause sensitivity and shouldn't be used all alone when ingested, although the amounts you're likely to use in cooking are safe. Add it *as a small proportion* to other ingredients in your preparations.

Magical It's said to repel snakes. Maybe they don't like the smell, or perhaps the grass is too tough to slither through. As with the medicinal use, add it in a small proportion to other ingredients in potions for lust; or to cleanse and open psychic channels.

Grow It Yourself Native to the tropics (possibly Sri Lanka and India), it requires full sun, rich, well-drained soil and a moderate amount of moisture. If you live in a cold zone, plant it in a *large* pot that you can bring indoors in the winter. Seeds are available but it grows easiest by root ball division. Or if you get a whole plant, including the base, from the grocery store, snip the leaves about two inches from the base and put the base in a dish of water (similar to the way celery can be grown from the trimmed base of a stalk). It should start rooting in about a week. Transplant to soil when the roots are three or more inches long.

Notes

LIME

Citrus laterifolia

"You put the lime in the coconut you drank 'em bot' up [...] Put the lime in the coconut, then you'll feel better." Did I just give you an earworm? More than forty years later, the recipe in the song holds true. Lime was used to prevent scurvy (as were lemons) and coconut water is, and always has been tasty, refreshing, and healthy.

Parts Used Fruit, juice, peel.

Cooking Limes are used like lemons but because they're stronger-flavored, require a smaller amount. You can find the juice and/or peel zest in recipes for fish, poultry, vegetables, salads and fruit. They add a refreshing tang to baked goods, the most famous preparation being Key Lime Pie. (Key limes are a hybrid that are a tart, even bitter cousin of the grocery store limes. The rind is thinner and they have many more seeds.) I prefer limeade to lemonade on a hot day.

Medicinal As mentioned above, the vitamin C content in limes will help treat scurvy. (Most citrus fruits will.) Like their lemon cousins, they are cooling and can be used as a substitute for lemon juice when treating sunburns (again, no sugar).

Magical Limes can be used in healing spells, or drink limeade as part of your ritual. Or, charge that limeade and give it to your lover to strengthen your bond. If you've been cursed or hexed, add lime slices (the number usually being 21) to a salt bath, rubbing yourself with each slice. Discard the slices after use. If you have a tree nearby, carry a twig or two to confer protection.

Grow it Yourself See "Lemon".

Notes

MARJORAM (SWEET)

Origanum majorana syn. *Majorana hortensis*

Often confused with its close cousin oregano, marjoram has its own place in the culinary, medicinal and magical worlds.

Parts Used Leaves, flowering tops.

Cooking Usually used fresh, marjoram is a natural for beef or game dishes such as stews. Don't forget that it can be used to season vegetables, fish, and chicken. Make a rub of it for your roasted poultry; add a pinch to your omelet; or combine with melted butter and sauté vegetables.

Medicinal Often used as a calming herb to treat anxiety or insomnia, it's also considered uplifting and is used to help depression. A cup of tea a couple of times a day may help with digestive issues such as indigestion, nausea, flatulence, constipation or diarrhea. It's also antibacterial and antiviral and may help with food poisoning, staph or other infections, the common cold or flu. More research is needed but it's thought one of its chemical constituents could be used to help diabetes and possibly some types of cancer.

Magical Use it to cleanse, purify and dispel negativity. For either insomnia or to help dreams, add it to a dream pillow. It can be added to mixtures for protection as well as drawing either love or wealth. Garlands of marjoram crown the bride and groom in many weddings or handfastings to ensure marital happiness. It's said growing a marjoram plant in a pot will confer safety to the home.

Grow It Yourself While a cousin of oregano, its growing conditions are somewhat different. Marjoram is an annual in most climates because, even mulched, it doesn't like any cold or excessive heat. In hot climates (as in south Florida), marjoram will be a *winter* annual. It prefers full sun and moderately moist soil. It does not tolerate overly-dry conditions at all. It is slow to germinate and slow to grow so either start it early indoors or buy a plant at your local nursery. If you already have a plant, you can take cuttings off it for a potted indoor plant in the winter, or divide the plants as they become too large for their spot.

Notes

MARSHMALLOW

Althea officinalis

No, this isn't the white, puffed, gooey sugar treat you see at the grocer's *but* it is the progenitor for that treat! It is also used as a glue and the seeds are used in furniture oils and varnishes.

Parts Used Flowers, leaves, root.

Cooking There are recipes out there to make the vegan version of marshmallows but it's most famous as an ingredient of Sirop de Guimauve, which is used in place of a sugar syrup in sweet cocktails such as daiquiris or Tom Collins. The leaves can be chopped finely and added to salads or used as a potherb or to thicken soups and stews. The roots can be boiled, sliced, and then fried with onions. The water used for cooking any part of the herb can be used in place of egg whites to thicken preparations such as meringues.

Medicinal Marshmallow is most famous for its demulcent qualities – it soothes and helps break up and expel mucus. So, use it for bronchitis, laryngitis, coughs of any kind, and inflammation of the respiratory, alimentary or urinary tracts. Demulcent is a term used to describe its actions internally – emollient is probably a word you already know for skin preparations. The same soothing qualities make it useful for insect bites, rashes and chapped skin. **Caution:** May interfere with the absorption of other drugs. There is anecdotal evidence of allergic reactions and lower blood sugar.

Magical Any part of the plant is protective and can be used to enhance psychic powers. Burn as an incense or carry with you in a sachet.

Grow It Yourself Marshmallow is a perennial, growing up to four feet high and two feet wide. It isn't picky about its soil (it will grow in almost anything from sand to clay with just about any pH level) but it will not grow in shade so be sure to plant it in a spot that gets at least partial sun. Sow it directly in late summer or early fall, or cold-stratify it for three to four weeks before planting outdoors in mid- to late spring. It probably won't flower until its second year and although the rule of thumb is to harvest roots in the second year, marshmallow roots probably won't be large enough to harvest for three or four years.

Notes

MEADOWSWEET

Filipendula ulmaria

Did you know? The old botanical name for meadowsweet was *Spiraea ulmaria*. Pronounce that first word and you'll see where the drug, aspirin, got its name.

Parts Used Aerial.

Cooking The whole plant is aromatic and slightly sweet with an almond-like finish, lending itself well to desserts, salads, ices, jellies and fruit dishes. It's strong, so a little goes a long ways. The flowers frequently flavor mead, beer, wine and cordials.

Medicinal Often used to ease the pain of heartburn, gastritis and peptic ulcers, it will also calm nausea. A small piece of the fresh root can be chewed to relieve headaches. **Caution:** Should be avoided by people with a salicylic acid sensitivity.

Magical Its sweet smell made it a favorite strewing herb in ancient times and today it can be strewn throughout the house and then swept up to instill happiness, peace and harmony in the home. Place fresh flowers on an altar as an offering during love spells or add the dried ones to mixtures for love or friendship sachets or incenses. Either the fresh or dried plant may be used in employment rituals.

Grow It Yourself Meadowsweet is a water-lover so it's an ideal plant for boggy areas, damp meadows, or next to water features in a landscape. You should start it from seed indoors and gradually harden off the seedlings before transplanting them outdoors well after the last frost. It likes *rich* soil and will be happiest if you give it at least one treatment of manure compost each year. Be sure you give it enough room – it will grow up to four feet high by over a foot wide. It will readily self-seed and those tufty seeds will float all over so to control the spread, remove the flower heads as soon as they're spent. Meadowsweet will easily crowd itself out so divide your plants every three to four years.

Notes

MUGWORT

Artemisia vulgaris

At one point in history, it was thought that wearing a sprig of mugwort or growing it near your house would ward off witches. *Then* it was thought if you had mugwort growing in your garden, you were a witch. The latter is probably closer to the truth – I know few witches who don't adore this herb.

Parts Used Leaves, root.

Cooking Rarely used in modern cuisine, at one time the young leaves and shoots were used as a condiment for goose, duck, pork, mutton and eel dishes; in China the leaves wrapped glutinous rice dumplings that were eaten during the Dragon Boat Festival. Mugwort is used as a potherb and to flavor rice cakes in Japan. Martha Stewart even has a mugwort soup recipe. At one time, it was used to flavor beer.

Medicinal As a bitter tonic and stimulant, mugwort can help a sluggish digestion. Conversely, it's also a nervine and may be helpful to calm nerves during stressful times. In Asian traditions, mugwort is used in moxibustion. **Caution:**

Mugwort contains thujone, which can be dangerous in large amounts or taken over long periods of time. It can also be a uterine stimulant to some women so should not be used during pregnancy. It is also a member of the *Asteraceae* family so may provoke an allergic reaction in those sensitive to those plants.

Magical This is where mugwort really shines. It is specific for dream magic, astral travel or to strengthen psychic powers. Add it to baths, put a sprig under your pillow or place in a sachet kept near you at night.

Roman soldiers put mugwort in their sandals to protect their feet from fatigue and this has carried over to putting it in modern shoes to gain strength during long walks or runs. Doing the same or pinning a sprig inside your clothing will protect travelers on long trips.

Use a mugwort infusion to cleanse crystal balls or other scrying tools.

Grow It Yourself Mugwort needs cold stratification so either dampen and refrigerate your seeds for a couple of weeks or plant them directly outdoors *before* the last frost. It likes full sun, a fairly neutral pH soil and only moderate water. It is a hardy plant and will survive *most* winters, but USDA zones 4 to 8 are its favorite. You can propagate it by harvesting the seed heads or dividing the plants in the fall.

Notes

MUSTARD (BLACK/BROWN/WHITE)

Brassica nigra, B. juncea, B. hirta

We're not talking about the condiment you put on your burger. That's made from these pungent little seeds plus other ingredients. There are three types of mustard seeds: yellowish-white, brown and black. All three are in the *Brassica* genus and have similar uses.

Parts Used Seed.

Cooking In addition to the condiment that enhances your favorite burger, they are used frequently in meat rubs and pickling. By gently toasting them in a skillet for a few minutes, they lose a little of their bite and impart a nutty flavor and crunch to fish, salads and rice. You can also find them as an ingredient in many curries. The oil (expressed or distilled from the seeds) is the preferred oil to cook lamb in recipes from Kashmir and Punjab.

If you grow it yourself, you'll have ready access to the greens, which can be cooked like collard greens.

Medicinal An infusion of crushed seeds is helpful for bronchitis and fever. A poultice of bruised seeds may be used on chilblains (soothe the skin afterward with an application of olive oil). Or put a tablespoon of bruised seeds in one liter of hot water for a relaxing footbath. **Caution:** May cause skin irritation, especially on fair-skinned people.

Magical Due to its "hot" nature, use in spells to represent the fire element. That nature also translates to spells for courage or protection.

Like any small seed, it can be used in fertility spells.

It's said the yellow seed, carried as an amulet, will bring faith followed by success. Or bury them under a doorstep or threshold to prevent entry of negativity.

Grow It Yourself Mustard grows easily but prefers cooler temperatures so plant them about a month before the last frost. Mustard likes nutrient-rich soil. If you're growing just for the greens, you can leave the plants about an inch apart

– you will be harvesting before the leaves get too big. You'll need to do succession planting for greens. If you want seeds, thin your seedlings to about six inches apart. They require *good* watering – at least a couple of inches a week. Harvest once the leaves are yellowed and the seed pods are brown.

Notes

NETTLE

Urtica dioica

Nettle *verb*: to vex or annoy. Anyone who's come into contact with this plant fully understands how the name of the plant became a verb. All those little needle-like hairs! If you're handling fresh nettle, be sure to wear long sleeves and gloves!

Parts Used Aerial, root.

Cooking Young nettle leaves can be cooked and eaten just like spinach. (The sting leaves the nettles as soon as they're heated, whether in hot oil or boiling water.) They can also be cooked and tossed with pasta similar to kale and chard or chopped into small bits and used like parsley in omelets and sauces.

Medicinal Once upon a time, nettle leaves were used as a flail to ease the pain of arthritis. Personally, I think you just substituted one pain for another. Urticaria is a real thing – that's the technical term for hives and guess where the name came from? Instead, make an infusion or tincture and take that internally and use it as a wash to help that arthritis as well as eczema and myalgia. The leaves are diuretic and so chockfull of vitamins and minerals that nettle is considered an excellent spring tonic. An infusion is taken by some to help with urinary tract infections, although there are other herbs better for this. **Caution:** Using fresh leaves externally may cause urticaria. In addition, internal use may decrease the efficacy of anticoagulants.

Magical If there's someone you want to annoy for whatever reason, stuff a poppet with fresh nettle leaves. Depending on the wording of your spell, you can also do the same to return a hex or curse to the sender.

Burning the dried leaves will banish negativity and protect an area. Sprinkle either those ashes or the powdered leaves or root on yourself to lighten your spirit if you're down, or drink an infusion of the leaves during a ritual for the same purpose.

Some traditions use nettle in lust-inducing spells.

Grow It Yourself I wasn't aware until recently that people actually *cultivate* nettle! It grows wild where I live so I harvest some in the spring before my husband starts the mowing, directing him to leave one or two alone each year until they go to seed. If you're not lucky enough to have it growing wild, set aside a sunny plot for it a ways away from your other herbs – it will spread. Plant the seeds in rich, moist soil after last frost. Be sure to keep that bed moist – it's often found along stream banks so you know it likes like water. The plants can grow up to four feet tall with almost foot-long leaves but harvest your leaves while they're still only a few inches long. The bigger they get, the tougher they are.

Notes

NUTMEG

Myristica fragrans

What we know as nutmeg is the seed of the tree. The way more expensive spice, mace, is the red aril (sort of like a skin) covering the seed casing. They do taste similar yet different. Be aware that nutmeg and mace are toxic and large doses may cause not only a headache or stomach upset but hallucinations, tachycardia or possibly death. (It was the "high" of choice in Victorian society for this very reason — for those who could afford it, that is. Nutmeg was expensive in those days.)

This is one herb where I'll suggest you buy already-ground nutmeg rather than whole. The seed is rather large and doesn't lend itself well to grinding up just a "little bit," unless you have a specialized spice grater. In addition, except for the good luck charm mentioned below, I've not come across anything that uses the whole seed.

Parts Used Seed, oil.

Cooking Nutmeg is very prevalent in baking. It's also used in cheese sauces (specifically béchamel), spinach or other "greens" dishes and on baked squash. I like a sprinkle of it on my café latte or cappuccino.

Medicinal Nutmeg is mostly used as a stimulant for the digestive system, e.g., sluggish digestion, gastritis, and even appetite loss. It is used in combination with other herbs to calm nausea and vomiting. In an ointment, its warming properties are helpful for arthritic conditions. Add a pinch of ground nutmeg to facial scrubs to reduce acne and its associated scarring. This is another herb you can add to warm milk in the evening to induce sleep – just a pinch will do it.

Magical Carrying a whole nutmeg with you will serve as a good luck charm. Put a sprinkle in whatever you're doing to help strengthen your mind, especially if you're working on your psychic abilities. It's an ingredient in many health and wealth spells.

Grow It Yourself Do you live in a tropical environment, such as USDA zones 10 and 11? Good. You'll have better luck. Nutmeg likes rich, deep soil (roots will go down four feet or more) and plenty of sun but not blazing heat when the trees are young. Therefore, a partially-shady area is best. The young trees will die if temperatures get anywhere near freezing. Nutmeg also doesn't tolerate wind well so plant them near a windbreak.

Notes

OLIVE

Olea europaea

Is there anyone without a bottle of olive oil in their kitchen? I didn't think so. But there's so much more to this herb than using its oil as a salad dressing or frying agent.

You'll quite often see the abbreviation "EVOO" in recipes. This means "extra virgin olive oil" and is unrefined. It has the least amount of oleic acid and typical olive-oil flavor. It's considered the healthiest of the grades but does have a low smoke-point. Grocery-shelf "olive oil" is generally a blend of unrefined and refined oil and lacks the typical flavor.

Olive oil doesn't have a long shelf life. Whatever grade oil you use, use it for *everything* and use it up quickly.

Parts Used Leaves, oil.

Cooking As you probably know, olive oil can be used in place of virtually any vegetable oil when cooking. It does, however, have its own taste which may or may not lend itself well to your dish. The leaves are rolled and stuffed with various things in Greek and Italian cooking, or as part of a recipe called Anatra Muta alle Foglie d'Olivo (Muscovy Duck with Olive Leaves).

Medicinal Much has been made of the health benefits of olive leaf tea or extract in the last few years. The ancient Greeks would probably say "duh". The leaves are antiseptic, anti-inflammatory, a febrifuge (brings down fevers), and highly nutritious. An infusion of the leaves will ease the pain of burns, soothe nervous tension, calm the itch of insect bites and rashes and help bruises and strains heal faster. A *decoction* of the leaves will help reduce a fever. The oil is thought to help bring down high cholesterol and is *known* to help constipation. As with most oils, it will soothe dry skin.

Magical Many old formulae use olive oil as a fixative. (They obviously used their preparations quickly.) The oil can be used to consecrate incense burners and thuribles; in healing ointments; and in rituals designed to provoke lust in men.

Use the leaves to bring peace, healing, fidelity, fertility and protection. For a headache, inscribe Athena's name on a leaf and tie it over the painful spot with a scarf or ribbon.

Grow It Yourself Olives like a climate with mild winters and long, dry summers. While they require a little cold (around 45° F) to produce flowers, anything below freezing will eventually kill what is normally a long-lived tree. (Olive trees can live to 1,000 years or more.) They *despise* wet feet so your soil must be well-drained. Olives like nitrogen-rich and slightly alkaline soil.

You will need to choose a cultivar that not only suits your climate and soil but also depends on whether you want fruit or oil from your crop. Some cultivars will produce both but you won't get a high-quality product out of those. You will also need to know whether your cultivar is self-pollinating or not.

Like any other fruit tree, they do require almost constant attention due to pests.

Dwarf olive trees have become available in the last several years which means you could grow one in a pot in the house.

Notes

ORANGE

Citrus sinensis

Here I'll be talking about *sweet* orange – the kind you find in the produce department and is so delicious. There is also *bitter* orange (*C. aurantium*), which does have its uses but isn't very flavorful.

Parts Used Fruit, juice, oil, peel.

Cooking Apart from eating the fruit or drinking the juice, oranges are used to make marmalade; in poultry dishes (Duck à l'Orange, anyone?); they are paired with other fruits, especially cranberries, in relishes, breads, and other baked sweets; fresh fruit sections are added to green salads; the list of uses is endless.

Medicinal All citrus fruits, not just oranges, are high in vitamin C and therefore good to treat scurvy. In a more modern context, they can help dyspepsia and flatulence. As an anti-inflammatory, oranges (or their juice) are quite useful during a bout of bronchitis.

Magical Add the dried peel and/or flowers to love sachets – especially those for marital bliss. Add them to baths for the same purpose. The peel is added to powders, incenses and other mixtures for prosperity. The Chinese consider the orange a symbol of luck and fortune, so use orange in spells for business negotiations. For divination, ask a yes/no question while eating the fruit and count the number of seeds. If the number is even, your answer is 'no'; if the number is odd, you're in luck.

Grow It Yourself Oranges do well in moderate climates – like Florida, California, Spain and parts of the Middle East. They like plenty of sunshine and a *lot* of water. They are very susceptible to frost. Most commercial trees are seedlings grafted to rootstock but you can grow a tree from seed. You can plant it directly in the soil or place it between two pieces of paper towel but it needs to be kept moist until it germinates. Because of the oddities of oranges, you may get an infertile tree or one that's completely different than the parent.

Dwarf orange trees are available so you could grow one in a large pot indoors.

Notes

OREGANO

Origanum vulgare

This is an herb that can be confused with another…it's also known as marjoram *but* it's "wild" marjoram. What you see in the stores as marjoram is the "sweet" relative. Sweet marjoram's Latin binomial is *O. majorana*.

Parts Used Leaves.

Cooking Oregano is used in Mediterranean, South American and Cajun dishes. It can be found sprinkled on vegetables, beans, seafood and in stews. I like to add a bit to my scrambled eggs. Add a pinch to store-bought spaghetti sauce or pizza to make them more flavorful.

Medicinal Oregano is one of the overlooked children of the mint family, although oregano oil is gaining popularity during cold and flu season for its antiviral properties. It's a stimulant so is helpful for sluggish digestion and to start moving mucus out of your system during a cold or the flu. Some people find a cup of oregano tea helps dispel a tension headache. It's useful externally, too. A vinegar rinse made with oregano will help with dandruff; a poultice will bring down swelling and ease pain.

Magical To me, oregano is a "happy" herb. Use it in spells to promote happiness (especially if you're trying to dispel depression), for healing and to maintain health. It can be used in both food and spells to attract or keep love. Some traditions weave oregano into circlets for the couple to wear at handfastings. It can also be added to mixtures or sachets made for protection and money matters.

Grow It Yourself As a member of the mint family, oregano is quite easy to grow. Unlike other mints, it will easily start from seed but cuttings and root divisions are also possible. It likes full sun; well-drained and loose but not necessarily rich soil; and a moderate amount of water (let the soil dry out between waterings). To ensure a lush, bushy plant, trim seedlings to about an inch from the center six weeks after planting.

It lends itself well to container planting. Indeed, one of its common names is pot marjoram. Oregano will grow *very* well if planted with basil and is considered an ideal companion plant to tomatoes and peppers. The leaves are tastiest if picked just when blooms form. Picking leaves continuously may prevent the plant from flowering.

Notes

PARSLEY

Petroselinum crispum

I always thought of parsley as nothing more than a garnish on a fancy dinner plate. Imagine my surprise when I found out it was much more than that!

Parts Used Leaves, root, seed.

Cooking There are two main types of parsley: "regular" (curly leaves) and Italian (flat leaves). Curly is the original; Italian is *P. crispum var. neapolitanum*. Some say curly parsley has little to no taste (or is slightly bitter) and Italian is more robust but it really depends on the individual plant and its growing conditions. Add it in quantity as another fresh green to your salad or to perk up sauces, marinades, quiches and soups. Parsley loses its flavor quickly so if you're adding it to a hot dish, wait until the last few minutes of cooking. The stalks, which have a stronger flavor, can be used as part of a *bouquet garni* for homemade stock or bean dishes.

Medicinal Parsley is *really* diuretic, especially the seeds and root. It can be used for kidney stones but *not* inflammatory kidney disease. The same qualities may possibly help with arthritis, high blood pressure, coughs and dandruff. If you're using parsley in a medicinal context be sure to increase your water intake to ensure you don't get dehydrated! It's also an appetite stimulant. **Caution:** Parsley is high in vitamin K and as such, should be used sparingly by those on a blood thinning medication. The essential oil should only be used internally under the guidance of a certified aromatherapist. It contains chemicals which, if misused, may result in all sorts of problems, including but not limited to paralysis and fatty degeneration of the liver and kidneys.

Magical Cunningham said when parsley is eaten, it provokes lust and promotes fertility but if you're in love not to cut it – you'll cut (lose) your love as well. Eat it or use it in spells to increase strength after surgery and to restore a sense of well-being. A plant in the house will draw prosperity to the home. Pinch a piece of that plant and place it on plates of food to guard against contamination.

Both the ancient Greeks and Romans considered parsley a plant of death. It is still planted at burial sites as a sort of memento mori.

Grow It Yourself Parsley is *tough* to grow from seed but not impossible. Start your seeds indoors ten to twelve weeks before the last frost. They are slow germinators and you may not see any sprouts for a month. Some experts recommend soaking them overnight in water prior to planting. Your soil should be rich and moist. Although parsley will survive some cold temperatures, it's probably best if you don't transplant them outside until the soil is warm. Parsley likes partial to full sun. It is a biennial so be sure to let some of your plants go to seed the second year.

Notes

PEPPER

Piper nigrum

Everyone has pepper in their kitchen, right next to the salt. Did you know? White, green and black pepper are all off the same vine! The color depends on whether the drupe (the fruit) is ripe and how it's processed. The ripening and processing are how the distinct flavors come about. What we know as a peppercorn is simply the dried fruit.

Parts Used Fruit.

Cooking Most people are accustomed to a sprinkle of pepper on their food either right before or right after the sprinkle of salt. According to Wikipedia, pepper is the world's most traded spice, which tells you how much it's used all over.

Medicinal The use of pepper as a medicine goes back probably as long as Man has been using it to flavor his food. It's a well-known digestive stimulant and will help with flatulence and bloating. A decoction of the dried fruit can be taken to reduce a fever or calm nausea.

Pepper essential oil can be diluted and used to calm a toothache until you can get to the dentist. Or use the diluted oil as a massage for arthritic pain.

Ayurvedic medicine uses pepper to soothe sore throats and calm coughs.

If you're into reading historical texts, I'd ignore the passages that tell you to use pepper for eye complaints. Ouch.

Magical Combine ground *black* pepper with salt and sprinkle around your space to dispel negativity – especially that thought to be of an evil nature. Along the same lines, whole peppercorns (color doesn't matter) can be added to protective amulets, sachets or spell mixtures.

Note: I wouldn't recommend burning peppercorns. The resulting smoke can be an extreme eye irritant.

Grow It Yourself Do you live in a hot, humid, tropical climate? Then you may be able to grow this perennial. Pepper does *not* tolerate even light frost and needs a great amount of water to survive. It is a climber (but not a parasite) so ensure you plant it next to trees or give it a trellis.

Notes

PEPPERMINT

Mentha x piperita

Mint juleps, mojitos…

Parts Used Aerial.

Cooking You know mint pairs *very* well with chocolate, right? Forgetting dessert for a moment, add a few fresh leaves to a fruit salad. Any soup made with tomatoes, such as gazpacho, will be perked up with a few chopped leaves – the freshness compliments the acidity of the tomatoes. Cooked eggplant cubes tossed with chopped mint, yogurt, garlic and cayenne is tasty. Then there's always the old standby – mint jelly in a lamb dish. Or mint jelly on toast for a wake-me-up breakfast.

Medicinal My list of therapeutic actions is twenty strong. Peppermint tea can be drunk nearly as often as desired to help with colds, flatulence, fever, flu, tension headaches, measles and nausea. This includes the nausea associated with morning sickness. Some find it a stimulant so although it's indicated for insomnia, you'll have to see how *your* body reacts to it. The diluted essential oil can be used in massage oils, rubbed on the gums of teething babies or where *you* have a toothache, or apply a couple of drops of the diluted oil to your temples or the nape of your neck for a tension headache. **Caution:** There are some drug interactions, so be sure to check. Research suggests drinking peppermint tea may inhibit testosterone and sperm production in humans so should not be drunk in quantity by men who are part of a couple trying to conceive. Peppermint is also contraindicated in cases of bile duct occlusion, gallbladder inflammation and liver damage.

Magical Like its list of medicinal uses, peppermint is good for *so many* things magical. Use it in spells to promote healing, attract love and for purification. Peppermint will enhance psychic powers and is specific for dream magic. A cup of tea before bed is recommended but again, it can be stimulating to some. Otherwise, put a sprig under your pillow or combine it with other things in a dream pillow. Rub the fresh herb or some diluted essential oil on furniture and floorboards to cleanse an area of negativity or just to raise the vibrations in that space.

Grow It Yourself Peppermint is *tough* to grow from seed. If you want to try, start them indoors mid-winter, transplanting the seedlings outside well after the last frost. The easiest method is to buy plants at your nursery. It likes moist soil and full-to-partial sun but does not like the extreme heat and sun of more southerly climates so in any zone above USDA 7, be sure to plant it in partial shade. Once established, peppermint is a hardy perennial that will spread quickly via its root system and choke out other plants. Therefore, give it its own bed or keep it in pots.

Notes

RICE

Oryza sativa

A commercial jingle just popped into my head but I don't want to pay the royalty fee so I won't inflict it on you.

Wild rice isn't really wild, nor is it the same species as regular rice, although they are cousins.

Rice is the world's third-largest commodity and provides more than one-fifth of the calories consumed worldwide.

Parts Used Oil, seed.

Cooking As a side dish, in a casserole, the uses are endless. Rice oil (extracted from the bran) has a high smoke point and a light flavor, making it ideal for stir-fries.

Medicinal There's an ongoing debate about the health benefits of brown rice versus white rice. White has had the bran (the brown outer hull) removed, which also removes some healthful compounds. Most white rice today is sold "enriched," meaning the manufacturer has added nutrients back in. White rice has a higher glycemic index than brown so may not be as good a choice for diabetics. Beyond that, there's not a *lot* of difference between the two. Rice aids calcium absorption, so is a good addition to a meal for people battling arteriosclerosis or high cholesterol. Either boiled rice or just the water rice has been boiled in are easily digested during bouts of indigestion or other stomach upsets.

Magical All those little seeds are a perfect indication that rice is used in fertility spells. For this reason it's thrown at the bride and groom at weddings. Despite rumors to the contrary, it's okay to do this – you won't kill any birds.

Add it to money spells. One suggestion I read is to half-fill a jar with rice, adding a few grains every day to increase wealth.

Throw rice into the air as part of a ritual to call rain.

A bowl of raw rice will absorb negativity in an area, or keep an open jar near your door to prevent negativity from entering. Replace the bowl or jar weekly, feeding the old rice to your neighborhood birds.

If you're good with very fine work, carve a protective symbol on a single grain of rice to carry with you. (You may cook the first hundred or more attempts.)

Grow It Yourself Do you have a marsh, a swamp, or at least a low-lying field that floods regularly? Then you may be able to grow rice. Start your seeds indoors, then transplant them to your chosen field a month or two later, or broadcast the seeds in a wet field. You'll want to ensure their feet stay *wet* – your water level should stay approximately three inches deep during the growing season. Rice matures in three to four months.

Notes

ROSE

Rosa spp.

"[…] that which we call a rose / By any other name would smell as sweet […]" (Shakespeare, *Romeo and Juliet*, Act II, Scene II.)

Parts Used Flowers (actually, the petals); hips (fruit).

Cooking First and foremost, be sure the roses you're using have *not* been sprayed with pesticides or fungicides! Once you've assured yourself of that, fresh rose petals can be crystallized as candy or cake decorations. Layer fresh petals with sugar to make rose-flavored sugar. Petals (or the essential oil) are an ingredient in the treat Turkish Delight. Add them to puddings, jams, or even cakes.

Fresh or dried petals can be ground and added to spice mixtures which can then be used as a rub on chicken, lamb or quail; and they're an ingredient in many rice dishes, especially those from the Middle East.

Use a rose hydrosol (flower water) in place of plain water when making any sweet.

The hips are used to make jam or as a healthy infusion. They are also the main ingredient in an alcoholic drink from Hungary called Palinka, as well as a favorite soft drink in Slovenia.

Medicinal An infusion of rose, while not specifically a calming herb, is known to ease the pain of a tension headache. Depending upon the reason, the same tea may help a bout of dizziness. John Lust recommended a wine decoction of rose for mouth ulcers, uterine cramps, toothache and earache.

Rose hips are high in vitamin C but the vitamin content varies not only between species but also individual plants. A rose hip syrup is a tasty way for children to get this vitamin. Rose hip harvest was encouraged in Britain during World War II because the Germans were sinking commercial ships, making importation of citrus fruits difficult.

Rose hip seed oil is pressed from the hips of specific species of rose (R. *canina*, R. *moschata* or R. *rubiginosa*) and is used not only in cosmetics but also in preparations to treat dermatitis, acne and eczema.

Magical According to the language of flowers, each color has a different meaning so bear this in mind when formulating your spells. Red means romantic love; white signifies purity and innocence; yellow is for friendship and joy; pink is gratitude and appreciation; orange, enthusiasm and desire; and finally, purple (especially dark), enchantment and love at first sight. Black roses are not naturally occurring so do not have a traditional symbolism. If, for some reason, you find a need for a *real* black rose (rather than darker-than-dark purple), put the stem in a glass of black ink for about a day.

Apart from its traditional use in love spells (and this can include the type of love you have for a friend), rose is also useful for healing, divination, protection (the thorns!) and psychic powers. Use them in baths, incenses and potpourri. The hydrosol (flower water) can be drunk alone or added to other potions.

Grow It Yourself The vast majority of the bushes on the market today (there are over 2,000 varieties) are cultivated for their looks rather than aroma. If you need or want the stronger aroma and/or flavor, be sure to search for "heirloom roses." These aren't quite as pretty but smell spectacular.

Starting a rose from seed (they're found inside the hip) requires a *lot* of patience. Most species need cold stratification; some won't germinate until they've gone through two "winters."

Ask your local nursery or field extension office which will grow best in your climate *and* in the spot you want to put it in (size varies from the low-growing moss-roses to climbers that will go ten to fifteen feet up). As a general rule, roses like full sun, a rich but well-drained soil, and quite a bit of water. They are also heavy feeders so *need* fertilization, no matter what soil you plant them in.

Roses are also very prone to disease (like fungi) and pests (like aphids). Growing roses organically is not for an otherwise busy person – they require a *lot* of attention.

Notes

ROSEMARY

Rosmarinus officinalis

Most people's introduction to this herb is when they're studying Shakespeare in high school and get to Hamlet. "There's rosemary, that's for remembrance," says Ophelia. Ol' Will wasn't wrong in his statement. The ancient Greeks knew (and modern science is now confirming) that rosemary does indeed help with memory. As a person who has "senior moments," I employ this herb a *lot*.

Parts Used Leaves, twigs.

Cooking Because it's a native of the Mediterranean, it can be found in many dishes from that region. It does best with root vegetables; in soups and stews; and with poultry, pork and lamb. There's even a suggestion to flavor lemonade with rosemary. If you can get them, fresh stems make wonderful kebab sticks.

Medicinal Rosemary's scent is reminiscent of pine and many people find it uplifting so it's a useful antidepressant. I add a few rosemary leaves when I'm steeping a cup of tea for anything of a viral nature, like the flu. It's not specifically antiviral but has antimicrobial properties. Externally, use a rosemary ointment as a rub for the pain of neuralgia and sciatica. (It will redden the skin but all that's doing is bringing blood to the surface capillaries.) That same ointment will help overworked muscles.

Magical Rosemary is a powerful cleansing, purifying and protective herb. I use it in place of white sage when smudging and add it to my magical washes. Use an infusion to wash your hands prior to doing any healing work.

Follow Ophelia's advice and add it to any spell to strengthen mental powers – it's great for studying!

It's said that inhaling rosemary's fragrance will preserve youthfulness. As a matter of fact, an entry on rosemary in an herbal from 1560 states: "Also make the a boxe of the wod & smell to it and it shall preserve thy youthe."

Grow it in your garden or in a pot on your deck if you're feeling insecure as a female. There are several old English sayings related to rosemary and they're all along the lines of "where rosemary grows, the woman rules the house." It's said men would secretly damage a flourishing rosemary plant because of this. Take advantage of this herb's strengths!

Grow It Yourself Rosemary is a perennial native to the Mediterranean and therefore likes to be warm and a little dry. Although it will tolerate partial shade, it will take all the sun it can get.

I have never seen rosemary seeds. Buy a plant at the nursery or get a friend to take a cutting for you off their plant. As a woody shrub, rosemary cuttings will easily root. Seedlings should be planted at least three feet apart after the last frost. They won't grow much in the first year (they're establishing their roots) but will take off in the second.

If you live anywhere it gets below freezing, either keep it in a pot you can bring indoors or be sure to cover it. Mine will tolerate a couple hours of below-freezing temperatures but no more than that.

In dry climates, mulch it to preserve moisture around the roots but do not mulch the crown of the plant to prevent rot. In wetter areas (or for those in pots), don't mulch at all and, if possible, allow the dirt to dry out completely between waterings. (Mother Nature doesn't always cooperate, does she?)

Notes

RUE

Ruta graveolens

Perhaps the bitterest herb there is (worse than wormwood, in my estimation), rue has fallen out of favor in recent years. However, it *does* have its uses.

Parts Used Aerial.

Cooking Its natural bitterness is moderated by acids so rue is a good addition to pickled vegetables, herbal vinegars and salads. A small branch may be added while simmering Italian tomato-based sauces (remove before serving). It goes well with bread, capers, cheese, chicken and eggs. One recipe makes a sauce with damson plums, red wine and rue to be served with meat.

Medicinal Pliny the Elder (23-79 CE) mentions eighty-four remedies with rue as an ingredient so you know it's been around a while. Today, its most common use is as a bitter. (Bitters are used to curb sugar cravings, stimulate digestion, soothe gas and bloating, support healthy liver function and to regulate bowel function.) As *bitter* as they are, chew the fresh leaves or drink a cup or two of an infusion to relieve a tension headache. An effective massage oil can be made by infusing the herb in a base oil. **Caution:** Rue is an emmenagogue, meaning it will stimulate menses. It should *never* be used in any way by pregnant women. The essential oil is a powerful abortifacient. There are also reports of toxic hepatitis and multi-organ failure due to rue use. Also, some people experience contact dermatitis when touching the fresh plant.

Rue is a well-known insect repellant and is grown in gardens for this purpose. The aroma is also repellant to many dogs and cats.

Magical Rue is best known as protection from the evil eye. A cimaruta (an Italian protective charm usually hung over an infant's cradle) is made from rue and, now, other herbs. Originally it was just rue … *clma di ruta*: sprig of rue.

Wear a sprig of rue to speed healing, whether from illness or injury. It can be added to poppets for the same purpose. Add it to incenses or use it as an asperger to sprinkle salt water around the home for purification and protection or to break hexes or curses.

Use rue in spells to break not only hexes or curses but bad habits.

Grow It Yourself Rue does best in a sunny location with well-drained soil. The soil doesn't have to be rich – it'll grow in rocky areas where nothing else will. Surface-sow seeds well after the last frost – they'll germinate in two to four weeks if they get plenty of warmth and sun. The plants will do well without a lot of attention and will even survive most drought conditions. They can grow more than three feet tall and are often planted as hedges in USDA zones 4 to 9.

Notes

SAGE

Salvia officinalis

There are so many varieties of sage that we'll stick with common sage. This is the same herb you put in your turkey stuffing, not the one shamans use. But, like many other plants, it contains thujone, which can be toxic in large doses and cause visions.

Parts Used Leaves.

Cooking I've already mentioned turkey stuffing. It goes well with other poultry, too, and in cheese and vegetable dishes.

Medicinal Sage is one of the go-to herbs when you need something dried up. Mothers who are trying to wean a baby will find it helpful as will those whose fevers have gotten to the sweating stage (but not while it's still a dry fever).

Those suffering from hyperhidrosis (excessive sweating) may find both drinking and rinsing the affected areas with a sage tea will aid drying.

Sage's antibacterial properties make it a good addition to mixtures for combating respiratory infections, sore throats, and even tonsillitis.

The tea is used as a wash prior to binding wounds – it will help cleanse the wound and stop bleeding.

Because of the high thujone content, instead of drinking a whole cup of sage tea three times a day, four to six tablespoons each time is all that is recommended.

Magical It's a sage. Therefore, it's good for purification and protection. If you don't have white sage, common sage will work just fine.

Although considered a masculine herb, from strengthening mental powers to promoting wisdom, it's great for women who want to hold their own in the world or just manage their household efficiently. So it's perfect for single mothers and/or women running their own business.

Write a wish on a sage leaf and keep it under your pillow for three nights. If the herb appears in your dreams, chances are your wish will come true. If you haven't dreamed of the herb in those three nights, bury the leaf in the ground to prevent anything bad happening.

The common name is also a clue to a use: sage = wisdom. Carry the herb (or a bit of the essential oil on a handkerchief) to improve your mental powers and to bring wisdom.

Grow It Yourself Again, we're talking about common sage. Sage will grow from seed but easier still is rooting a cutting from an existing plant. Easiest is buying a plant at the nursery. Plant your seedlings (whether purchased or those seeds you started indoors a couple of months earlier) a foot or so apart when your nighttime temperatures don't fall below 50° F. Sage is winter-hardy to USDA zone 5 but the youngsters need a little time to acclimate. It likes slightly sandy soil (well-drained) and full sun. Water babies frequently so they don't dry out. Adult plants can tolerate a little dryness. Although a perennial, experts suggest replacing your plants every five years or so to ensure the highest quality herb.

Sage makes a wonderful companion plant for rosemary, cabbage and carrots but will do nasty things to nearby cucumbers.

Notes

SPEARMINT

Mentha spicata

Of the two most popular mints (the other being peppermint), spearmint seems to be the unloved stepchild. You don't see it used as often as the other, which is a shame, really.

Parts Used Flowering tops, leaves.

Cooking Here, fresh leaves are best. You can use them in mixed drinks, green salads, fruit salads (pairs especially well with watermelon), Asian spring rolls, and many desserts.

Medicinal As a diaphoretic (makes you sweat) and diuretic, spearmint may be used to reduce fever and help with fluid retention and suppressed urine. For those who don't care for peppermint, it can be used to calm nausea (even morning sickness), indigestion and vomiting. A cup of tea may be calming to some, stimulating to others. Added to an ointment, it is cooling and calms the itch of hemorrhoids. **Caution:** See the notes under peppermint about decreased testosterone and sperm production. The essential oil is potent and used internally in excessive amounts may lead to gastrointestinal irritation and depression of the central nervous system.

Magical *So* helpful for healing spells, especially anything having to do with the lungs. Sometimes used to attract love, sometimes just lust. (Intention is everything!) Use the whole herb or essential oil in spells to strengthen mental powers – the aroma is what you're looking for. Kept around the bed, it will protect you while sleeping. Carry it with you to strengthen your convictions when dealing with an unpleasant situation.

Grow It Yourself Just like its cousin, spearmint is *tough* to grow from seed. If you want to try, start them indoors midwinter, transplanting the seedlings outside well after the last frost. The easiest method is to buy plants at your nursery. It likes moist soil and full-to-partial sun but does not like the extreme heat and sun of more southerly climates so in any zone above USDA 7, be sure to plant it in partial shade. Once established, spearmint is a hardy perennial that will spread quickly via its root system and choke out other plants. Therefore, give it its own bed or keep it in pots.

Notes

STAR ANISE

Illicium verum

When I first saw this spice as a child, I thought it was chocolate in the shape of a star. Imagine my surprise when I attempted to bite into it!

Parts Used Fruit, seed.

Cooking Although somewhat sweet in flavor, it's traditionally used in savory recipes, especially meats. Add it whole to soups, stews and braising broths (remove before serving). Star anise is a staple of Chinese and Indian cuisine. It's also utilized as a less-expensive substitute for anise in liquors and baking.

Medicinal An infusion of the fruit is a traditional remedy for rheumatoid arthritis. The seeds can be chewed to aid digestion; an infusion of the fruit also aids digestion, especially in cases of flatulence. The infusion is gentle enough for use in children with colic. Not that you should try this at home, but star anise is the primary source of the chemical compound used to make Tamiflu®.

Magical Traditionally, the seeds are used but the dried fruit will work as well. Burn it as incense to increase psychic powers. Carry or wear as a general bringer of good luck. From folklore: place it under your pillow at night to keep bad dreams at bay and also to dream of someone far away.

Grow It Yourself Indigenous to the tropical and subtropical regions of China, star anise will grow as a small tree in USDA zones 9 and 10 (you *may* be able to grow it as a houseplant in other zones). Start your seeds indoors, planting about one inch deep in good potting soil, then cover with plastic wrap (poking a few holes in it for air circulation) to keep everything moist and warm. After your seeds have sprouted, remove the plastic and keep the soil moist but not wet. Once your seedlings are about five inches tall, transplant them individually to a *large* pot that you keep protected from wind but still exposed to the sun. Keep the soil moist. In about three years, you'll have a sapling that will be strong enough to withstand planting outside in well-drained soil with full sun. You'll still have to wait a few years before the tree will produce fruit.

Notes

STRAWBERRY

Fragaria spp.

Those lovely, plump fruit you see at the grocery store are simply cultivars of the same plant that grew wild in my yard in Atlanta. (They're much larger and taste a *lot* better, too.)

Parts Used Fruit, leaves.

Cooking Naturally, sweets come to mind. Dip strawberries in melted chocolate for a decadent treat; make jam, shortcake and other desserts. Strawberry also pairs well with chicken (especially in green salads) and milder cheeses such as ricotta or goat.

Medicinal Slightly crush a fresh strawberry and rub it on a pimple. Your spot should disappear overnight. For problem acne, take an infusion of the leaves every day and use that same infusion as a rinse on your face. Do the same for mild cases of eczema. Strawberries (the fruit *or* an infusion of the leaves) will help with diarrhea and dysentery. If you make an infusion of the leaves, instead of the usual one teaspoon dried herb to one cup water, use *two* teaspoons leaves in *one-third* cup water.

Magical Strawberries are served as a love food (see my note above about dipping them in chocolate). The leaves are carried for luck; pregnant women also carry them (in a sachet) to ease the pain of pregnancy and childbirth. The fruit or leaves can be used in spells to attract good fortune and favorable circumstances.

Grow It Yourself I've never seen strawberry seeds (except on the fruit before I eat it). Buy plants of a type appropriate for your area at a nursery. Plant them in well-draining, loamy soil in full sun. (It's recommended that you work quite a bit of manure or compost into the dirt the season before planting.) Be sure to give them plenty of room because they grow by sending out runners which produce daughter plants, which then send out their own runners. Pluck the flowers off the first year so they don't fruit. If you don't, they won't establish good root systems and you'll end up with plants that don't produce a lot of fruit.

The root systems are shallow so ensure they get plenty of water. Weeds will also easily crowd out strawberries, so keep your beds mulched and weeded. After harvest, cut or mow the plants down to about an inch high and then heavily mulch until the following spring.

Notes

TEA

Camellia sinensis

Did you know? Black, green and white Tea are all off the same plant. What you see on the supermarket shelves as "white", "green", "oolong" or "black" Tea are all the same herb in a different phase of oxidation: the chlorophyll breaks down when exposed to air. White Tea is made of immature leaves and buds processed immediately after harvest; green Tea is wilted but hasn't been left to oxidize; oolong is wilted and partially oxidized; and black Tea is wilted and fully oxidized. Many of the American brands are "Orange Pekoe." This is a *grade* of black Tea and doesn't have any orange flavoring at all. Some think the "Orange" comes from when the Dutch (House of Orange) were the largest importers of Tea from China.

Parts Used Leaves.

Cooking There are so many varieties of Tea on the market that you'll have to rely on your own taste buds to decide which you want to use. Apart from a cuppa, use Tea to marinate meats and/or vegetables. You can grind the leaves and use them, along with other spices, as a meat rub. Steep a teabag in melted butter for a few minutes, remove the bag and pour the butter over vegetables, rice … any recipe you add butter to. Poach fruit in brewed Tea. Add ground leaves to your favorite cookie recipe – Earl Grey makes a wonderful shortbread. There are several types of Tea ice cream on the market. Tea sorbet is popular, too.

Medicinal Tea, especially white and green, contains powerful antioxidants, most notably ECGC (and the commercial packaging will remind you if you forget). Oolong and black don't have as much of this compound – oxidation destroys some of it.

Because of the antioxidants, Tea has been shown to reduce the risk of heart disease and many types of stroke. It does so by lowering cholesterol levels in the blood and preventing the buildup of fatty deposits on artery walls. Studies have shown that green Tea also helps reduce the risk of most types of cancer. It may also help with diabetes, osteoporosis, arthritis, eczema and even tooth decay. There is a study out suggesting that drinking green Tea may help with the memory problems associated with sleep deprivation caused by obstructive sleep apnea.

Tea is also astringent. I'm sure many women know that putting a couple of cold Tea bags over your eyes for about ten minutes will reduce under-eye puffiness. Soaking your feet in a strong Tea will get rid of food odor – the tannins change the skin's pH level, making it unfriendly to odor-causing bacteria. It's also great to ease the pain of a sunburn or to reduce the swelling and itching of a bug bite.

Caution: Tea *does* contain caffeine. (Even decaffeinated has a *little* left.) Overdoing your consumption may lead to gastrointestinal upset and nervous irritability.

Magical Tea makes a wonderful addition to all money spells and charm bags, or give a charged cup of Tea to someone who needs some extra courage or strength. The same cup of Tea can be used as a base for a lust-inducing drink.

It doesn't smell very good burning as an incense (at least I don't think so) but even Tea from commercial bags works very well.

Grow It Yourself Tea is a wonderful evergreen shrub (3 to 12 feet tall) and will grow nicely outdoors in zone 8 or higher, or you can put it in a (large) pot and bring it indoors for the winter. Be sure your soil drains well and place it where it gets some shade during the day. Yes, it's related to the camellia most of us know as a flowering bush and smells wonderful when blooming.

Notes

THYME
Thymus vulgaris

"Parsley, sage, rosemary and…" Many of you will have to google those song lyrics. Even if you don't think you do, google them anyways. You'll be surprised just how old that ballad is.

Parts Used Flowering tops, leaves.

Cooking Thyme is popular in Mediterranean, Cajun and Creole cuisine. It's mostly used with root vegetables and beans. I like it in some tuna dishes and it adds a little something to preparations with button mushrooms. (Those are the ones you find most often at the grocer's.)

Medicinal This is another herb with a list of uses a yard long. It's slightly drying (not as much as sage), is most definitely antiseptic and disinfectant… use it internally for colds and flu and the coughs associated with them; laryngitis, bronchitis, sore throats; and even to dry up diarrhea. Externally, use a tea as a wash for wounds or chilblains; in an ointment for arthritis and eczema. I've seen recipes for natural deodorants that include this herb.

Caution: While Generally Recognized as Safe (GRAS) in amounts used in cooking, it's been reported to affect the menstrual cycle so I'd avoid it if pregnant or nursing. It also contains thujone so read the cautions about that chemical constituent under "Sage."

Magical Go back to the long list of medicinal uses. Translate that: it's good for health, healing and purification.

Add it to baths to ensure a constant flow of money. Along the same lines, put it in a jar either at home or work to bring good luck.

A sprig under your pillow or a handful of leaves in a dream pillow will ensure restful sleep.

It's said that women who wear a sprig in their hair will make themselves irresistible. (Be careful where you place it. Those stems can be woody. You don't want to poke your man's eye out.) The same sprig should be worn to help you through grieving or to provide strength and courage where needed.

Grow It Yourself Thyme *will* grow from seed but the germination rate is irregular. Plants are readily available at garden centers or you can take a cutting off a friend's plant. To grow from seed, start them indoors six to ten weeks before your last frost date. Transplant seedlings or purchased plants outside when your soil is warm but not necessarily after last frost – the plants will survive a light frost.

Thyme likes full sun and well-drained soil but it's not too picky about the *kind* of soil. It's a hardy perennial and likes to be pruned/harvested a couple of times a year. I usually do mine about a month before flowering and then about a month after.

If your ground freezes in winter, be sure to mulch the plants well in the fall and then remove the mulch once the ground warms up. As a woody plant, it's susceptible to fungus and rot if kept continually wet.

Notes

YARROW

Achillea millefolium

Yarrow stalks are the traditional material used for I Ching divination. I see its use in your future...

Parts Used Aerial.

Cooking Who knew? Yarrow (the leaves) is very similar to tarragon and may be substituted for it, although its taste may be too powerful for some people. Like any other soft herb, don't *cook* it, but add it at the very end if you're sautéing meat or vegetables. It does quite well in cold preparations where things are "perfumed" or marinated with herbs. One site I read theorized using yarrow instead of dill would make a tasty gravlax. Combine it with a blander herb, say, parsley, in a vinaigrette.

Medicinal According to *The Iliad*, Achilles' soldiers used yarrow to heal their wounds, hence the genus name. Being a klutz, yarrow is my go-to herb for stopping bleeding. Of any kind. If you're out in the field and skin your knee, simply grab a handful of yarrow, crush it a bit and put it on the injury. The leaves aren't quite as soft as they appear and will feel scratchy, but they will do the trick. Be sure to wash your wound thoroughly when you can get real first-aid treatment to get all the bits and pieces out.

Apart from that, yarrow's astringency, diaphoretic and expectorant qualities make it a useful addition to teas for bronchitis, colds, coughs, and fevers. Add it to external preparations for hemorrhoids, candida, thrush and vaginal infections. **Caution:** Avoid using with other herbs containing thujone to prevent thujone toxicity. Excessive doses may interfere with anticoagulant, hypo- and hypertensive therapies. Because of the thujone content, use of yarrow should be avoided during pregnancy and nursing.

Magical In addition to adding it to *any* healing mixture, yarrow is said to draw love … use it in handfastings, over the (marriage) bed, or carry it with you to atttact friends or relatives with whom you want contact. Young girls in the Scottish Highlands cut it before sunrise, place it under their pillow and dream of their sweetheart. If he's facing them, marriage will follow. If his back is turned, it won't.

It's widely used in the Orkney Islands to dispel melancholy. Hang bunches of yarrow around the house to banish negativity and sadness.

Yarrow confers courage. Wear it for protection; hold a stalk in your hand to stop fear.

Add it to teas or incenses to increase psychic powers.

Grow It Yourself Yarrow is very easy to grow in almost any climate. Start your seeds indoors, or sow outdoors in late autumn or early spring when nighttime temperatures are still around 62° F. They'll pop in just a couple of weeks. Be sure not to cover your seeds as they need light to germinate. If you sow directly outdoors, purchase plants or replant seedlings, till your soil about a foot deep to give the rootlets plenty of room to spread and space your plants about a foot apart.

Yarrow likes full sun, only moderate water and doesn't really care about its soil type. It grows wild where I live and while I have a nice "carpet" of yarrow leaves in a shady spot, that patch does not put up stalks, much less flower.

Although not a member of the mint family, yarrow spreads just as fast and can be considered invasive. For best results, divide your plants every four or five years and cut everything back in autumn.

Notes

HONORABLE MENTION

Virtually every plant on this planet will do at least double duty. So many I know that I couldn't just end it on the previous page. If you have one of the below (or others), do some research – you'll find them useful!

Arrow root (Several different tropical species): Cooking, magical

Borage *Borago officinalis*: Cooking, medicinal, magical

Coconut *Cocos nucifera*: Cooking, magical

Dragon's Blood *Daemonorops draco*: Medicinal, magical

Echinacea *Echinacea angustifolia, E. purpurea*: Medicinal, magical

Feverfew *Tanacetum parthenium*: Cooking, medicinal, magical

Frankincense *Boswellia carterii*: Medicinal, magical

Myrrh *Commiphora myrrha*: Medicinal, magical

Oak *Quercus alba*: Cooking, medicinal, magical

Orris Root *Iris germanica var. florentina*: Cooking, medicinal, magical

Passionflower *Passiflora incarnata*: Cooking, medicinal, magical

Patchouli *Pogostemon cablin*: Cooking, medicinal, magical

Pennyroyal *Mentha pulegium:* Cooking (old), medicinal, magical

Plantain *Plantago major, P. lanceolata:* Cooking, medicinal, magical

Poppy *Papaver somniferum* (opium poppy), *Eschscholzia californica* (California poppy): Cooking, medicinal, magical

Sandalwood (white) *Santalum album:* Cooking (nuts), medicinal (bark and oil), magical (bark and oil)

Skullcap *Scutellaria laterifolia:* Medicinal, magical

St. John's Wort *Hypericum perforatum:* Cooking (schnapps), medicinal, magical.

Vervain *Verbena officinalis:* Medicinal, magical

Wintergreen *Gaultheria procumbens:* Cooking (berries), medicinal (leaves and oil), magical (leaves and oil)

Wood Betony *Stachys officinalis:* Medicinal, magical

Notes

www.ingramcontent.com/pod-product-compliance
Lightning Source LLC
Chambersburg PA
CBHW050631300426
44112CB00012B/1757